THE ATLAS OF HAPPINESS

The global secrets of how to be happy

Helen Russell

TWO
ROADS

First published in Great Britain in 2018
by Two Roads
An imprint of John Murray Press
An Hachette UK company

10 9 8 7 6 5 4 3 2 1

Text copyright © Helen Russell 2018
Illustrations by Naomi Wilkinson
Illustrations copyright © Two Roads

Some names and identifying features
have been changed to preserve
anonymity.

A CIP catalogue record for this title is
available from the British Library

Hardback ISBN 9781473688230
eBook ISBN 9781473688247
Audio ISBN 9781473688339

Typeset in Madera
Designed by Andrew Barron
@ Thextension

Printed and bound in Europe

Hodder & Stoughton policy is to use
papers that are natural, renewable and
recyclable products and made from
wood grown in sustainable forests. The
logging and manufacturing processes
are expected to conform to the
environmental regulations of the
country of origin.

Hodder & Stoughton Ltd
Carmelite House
50 Victoria Embankment
London EC4Y 0DZ

www.tworoadsbooks.com
www.hodder.co.uk

THE ATLAS OF HAPPINESS

CONTENTS

For the mini Vikings,
who have been waiting for a book with pictures.

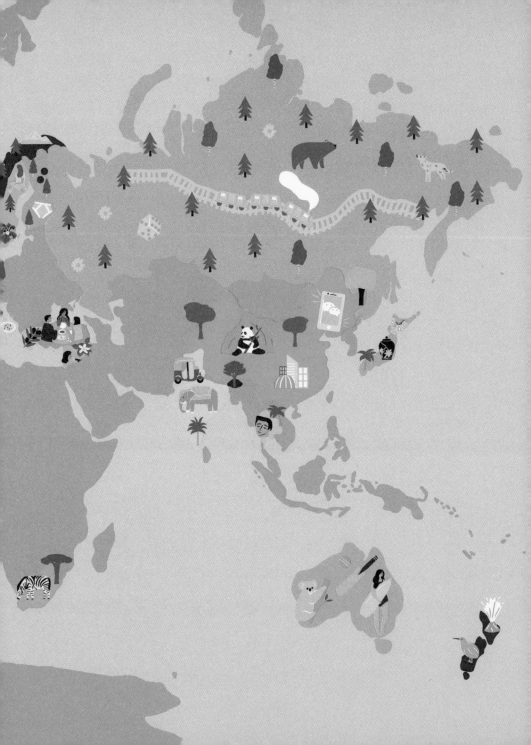

INTRODUCTION

elcome. Really. Come on in. It can be tough out there. It's easy to watch rolling news and get the idea that the world is getting more miserable by the minute. That we're all becoming more isolationist and that these are bleak times indeed. But news is about the 'stuff' that happens, not the 'stuff' that doesn't happen. It's not 'news' that life expectancy has never been higher, nor that leisure time has never been more bountiful, wherever you are.

No front pages will be dedicated to the fact that thanks to modern technologies, the amount of time spent doing housework has fallen from sixty hours a week to just eleven hours (all hail the spin cycle...). According to Millennium Development Goals data and the most recent World Bank report, in the past twenty-five years, world hunger has declined by 40 per cent, child mortality has halved and extreme poverty has fallen by two thirds – three statistics that are unlikely to be trending on Twitter any time soon.

When things are ticking along well, there's very little to report. Negativity bias means that, as human beings, we experience 'bad' events more intensely than we do the 'good' – and we also remember them more. But that doesn't mean that 'bad' is all there is. We have to work to consciously remember the 'good' and remain hopeful – or we can't make things better.

Optimism isn't frivolous: it's necessary. If we feel hopeless all the time, if we're always in crisis, the natural response is to give up and stop trying altogether. But we can't let snark win. Problems are there to be solved. Challenges, to be met. We can be aware of the bad whilst also being mindful of how we can make it better. There are people all around the world finding happiness every day, both in countries that top the global happiness surveys and in those that don't. By learning about them we can find more ways to be happy ourselves and help each other. Empathy is essential, and learning about what matters to people on the other side of the world helps us all. Understanding how different nations view happiness can impact on how we interact with one another going forward.

This book was inspired by the fascinating testimonies I've been privy to since I started researching happiness in 2013 for my first book, *The Year of Living Danishly*. Since then, I've been approached in some of the most bizarre settings (public toilets; forests; sand dunes...) by people from all over the world who want to share their own country's unique happiness concepts. As an international living overseas, I'm also privileged to have a delightfully diverse social circle, and confidantes from every continent have offered expertise and enlightenment. The result is a catalogue of cultural customs to give a horizontal perspective on happiness and what it means to live a good life around the world. The regions are in alphabetical order, to offer an unexpected and unusual tour through the different approaches adopted globally. This isn't a compendium of the world's happiest countries; instead it's a look at some of the concepts that are making people happier in different places. Because if we look exclusively at countries that are already coming top of the happiness polls, we miss out on a wealth of ideas and knowledge from cultures we may be less familiar with.

Nowhere is perfect. Every country has faults. These pages unashamedly celebrate the best parts of a country's culture as well as national characteristics at their finest – because that's what we should all be aiming for. The list of concepts won't be exhaustive and I'm open to learning more – if there's a happiness hack that I've missed, keep me posted. Little words can have a big impact and ostensibly simple ideas can change the way we look at the world. No one thought that *hygge* would catch on. Now it's a global phenomenon. You decide which of the concepts within these pages will be next.

Some of the themes that sprung out of my research were universal – such as time with family and friends, taking the pressure off at work, or engaging with nature – while others, like pants-drinking in Finland or appreciating ageing in Japan, were intriguingly unique. But one thing's for sure: we can all get happier, and there are endless possibilities for ways to try.

So here are 33 reasons to be cheerful: inspirations to keep you hopeful and to offer succour to anyone at the end of their tether. Some of the concepts will contradict others – just as the cultures of some countries appear the antithesis to those of their neighbours. That's OK: we're all different. Take what works for you. Read. Refuel. And go get 'em.

'Fair go', a phrase used to mean that everyone and everything is deserving of a reasonable chance. First recorded in the *Brisbane Courier* in 1891 when striking sheep shearers were arrested without having their warrants read to them first and demanded of their manager, 'Do you call this a fair go?' The strike was one of the earliest and most important in the country's history, spurring the birth of the Australian Labor Party and the perception of Australia as an egalitarian society, where fairness, good sportsmanship and a positive outlook are prized.

AUSTRALIA

The opening piano chords still trigger in me a Pavlovian response, transporting me to the endless summers of my youth and the beginnings of my education in beach life, surfing, and the spirit of 'fair go'. As a child growing up in 1980s British suburbia, the first two were of little use, but the third gave me a grounding in what I like to think are my liberal leanings today. I was six years old and *Neighbours* was airing for the first time. The Australian soap opera's cheery G and C major intro (a lot like The Carpenters' 'Close to You') marked the start of a fifteen-year daily pilgrimage to Ramsey Street. When *Home and Away* reached the UK in 1989, I watched that, too. Which means that between the impressionable ages of six and twenty-one (I was at university, what else was I going to do?) I had 3,510 hours of 'tutorials' on 'no worries' Australian sunshine culture and the 'fair go' philosophy.

This was time well spent, according to my friend Sheridan from Brisbane. Because friendliness, sunshine and the spirit of 'fair go' are what makes Australians tick – so as an amateur anthropologist and happiness researcher, I was simply starting early.

'"Fair go" is really important for happiness in Australia and it means equality of opportunity and giving everyone a fair shot,' says Sheridan. Gen, a friend from Adelaide, agrees: 'It means that no matter where you're from or who you are, if you can do the job, there should be no reason why you can't – and this extends to saying you'll give something a "fair crack", like you'll give it your best try.' This, in turn, makes you happy – because there's a feeling that everything is achievable, everyone's equal, and you're all in it together.

Australia regularly ranks among the top ten happiest countries worldwide and Aussies have always been known as an upbeat, friendly bunch. They learn from an early age to get along, 'play the game' and 'participate' above all else. 'Teachers are fixated on this,' says Ben, from Melbourne, ' – and everyone is encouraged to take part. I remember at school there were as many left-handed pairs of scissors as there were right-handed ones in the classroom. I always got stuck with the green-handled left-handed ones...'

But the Australian ideal of giving it a 'fair go' is most evident when it comes to the country's national obsession: sport. Ben has fond memories of being hauled out of a football match one day for having his arms folded. 'I told my coach, "I thought I was doing OK!" but he told me, "No: you were just standing there, you weren't giving it a fair go!" You have to try – that's the thing,' says Ben. This is more important than demonstrating any natural aptitude and all Australian schoolchildren grow up playing netball or football in winter and cricket in summer.

'Cricket is the closest thing we have to a religion in Australia,' says Ben, which is why the national team's 2018 ball-tampering scandal knocked the knees out from under many Aussies. The International Cricket Council gave the Australian team a one-game suspension but Cricket Australia – the national association – decided to observe a one-year suspension. 'We punished ourselves far more harshly than the rest of the world did,' says Ben (Ben works in marketing, but still, when it comes to the Australian cricket team, it's 'we'). I remark that the offence of 'sandpapering a ball' seems so mild in these days of doping scandals and dubious urine samples, but Ben assures me it was A Big Deal. 'Cheating is completely against the Australian values of playing fair – where everything has to be just and equal,' he says, 'so yes, there was crying on national TV about what they'd done. Because they broke the "fair go" code.'

Sports are so revered in Australia that there's a public holiday before the Australian Football League Grand Final in Victoria and everyone gets the day off for the Melbourne Cup. 'We also love rugby (League & Union), swimming, tennis...' says Liz, my old flatmate, who comes from Perth, '– and you don't need to be good at sport personally to worship it.' We all know that taking part in sports can make us happier and healthier by releasing endorphins – but being a sports fan has been proven to make us happier, too. Fandom gives us a sense of community and this 'belonging' boosts our well-being. Sports psychology researchers from Murray State University in the US found that sports fans reported higher levels of general happiness, lower levels of loneliness and a markedly better social life, as well as a common language with which to communicate. Something Australians seem to have cottoned on to years ago. Ben tells me how sporting clubs in Australia take new migrants to football games so that they can get to know the culture and have something to talk to their new colleagues or classmates about. 'It's that important,' he stresses. But interestingly, there's not the same level of tribalism or exclusivity involved in supporting a sports team in Australia as you might find in other countries. 'We're all about the underdog,' says Sheridan: '– so we'll always back them, because otherwise that's not fair and it could be you one day. As long as the other team are having a fair crack at it, they deserve a "fair go". It's like our national motto.'

Of course, the reality doesn't always measure up to the rhetoric and some have demonstrably not had a 'fair go' historically – like Australia's Aboriginal people, who have been systematically discriminated against in practically every way imaginable since the British colonisation of Australia began in 1788. As Sheridan says: 'Australia definitely has blinkers about Indigenous Australians.' 26 January is still marked as 'Australia Day' in 'honour' of the First Fleet's landing, although many Australians are now in favour of renaming it 'Invasion Day'. Australia hasn't always been great on LGBTI rights, either, despite Sydney's reputation as one of the world's most gay-friendly cities. But in 2017 Australians voted in huge numbers for marriage equality to give a 'fair go' – finally – for love. And in March 2018, the Northern Territory was the last jurisdiction to pass an adoption equality law to allow same-sex adoption.

Today, the right to a 'fair go' has been found to be Australians' highest rated value in a survey published in Victoria's state newspaper, *The Age*. A consequence of this is that Australian society aspires to be stridently anti-hierarchical. No one is better than anyone else, so why should they be treated differently? There's an anti-authoritarian streak in every Australian and a hallmark of Aussie comedy is the pricking of pomposity (*Kath & Kim* and *Utopia* are two of my favourite TV exports. I've finally moved on from *Neighbours*...). This attitude has led to a riotously raw turn of phrase that distinguishes Australian English from the language used by their more repressed cousins on the other side of the world *waves*. There's nothing guaranteed to cheer up a morning more than remembering the delightfully surreal Australian adage: 'He's got a few roos loose in the top paddock...' – meaning that the kangaroos in someone's brain have gone AWOL and they are therefore lacking in intellect. Or the wonderfully earthy: 'We're not here to fuck spiders...' used to imply: 'We're not here to mess around and should probably get on with the task at hand.' Which, we can all agree, isn't half so much fun to say out loud.

'I think we're pretty good at laughing at ourselves,' says Sheridan, 'and we don't take ourselves too seriously. We have a positive outlook on the whole but we're laid-back about it.' Because: 'no worries'. This is an expression used everywhere now – from the US to the UK, New Zealand, South Africa and even Canada – but 'no worries' epitomises Aussie culture, summing up a friendly gregariousness, a robust jocularity and a casual optimism.'"No worries' is wired into the Australian psyche,' says Ben, 'it's a way of thinking that suggests, no matter how bad things are, "she'll be right" – another of our phrases – in the end. There's a lot of hope. And confidence.' Despite, I point out, the fact that Australians have plenty of things to worry about in reality – from sharks to jellyfish, snakes, crocodiles, 'scorpion fish' (a thing, apparently) and deadly spiders (fucked or otherwise...). *You're not worried about any of these?* I ask, tentatively. Ben shrugs. 'I mean, we're all going to die anyway...' is his response. 'But it's like "no worries" is a creative brief that allows me to live and love fearlessly, even if it doesn't always work out.'

As a chronic worrier, the idea of a 'no worries' approach to life appeals. Living by this mantra in a country that doesn't have deadly creatures hiding under every rock should be a breeze. But how to stay positive on those days when everything just seems too hard? 'The sunshine helps,' says Sheridan. 'It keeps you level, mood-wise, and you've got these bright blue skies.' Cases of seasonal affective disorder (SAD) – the clinical condition believed to be caused by decreased light exposure in winter – are extremely rare in Australia where sunshine reigns. Mostly. 'But even when we get tropical storms,' Sheridan reflects, 'the heavy rain isn't cold.' I remember getting caught in a thunderstorm in Sydney years ago that just felt like a pleasantly warm power shower. That's right: even the rain's agreeable in Australia. Sheridan consoles me in my life-envy slightly by telling me that the perennially sunny forecast can throw up its own difficulties: 'Life's a beach in Australia – or at least, you're there a lot of the time. And it's 36 or 38 degrees in Queensland. And I have freckled white skin. I spent the first sixteen years of my life in board shorts, a full rash vest and a hat. Sometimes I carried an umbrella for shade, too. I looked like an 18th-century lady crossed with Bart Simpson...'

I sympathise, I tell her: my skin doesn't like the sun either. But my soul really does. Ben gets this: 'There's nothing like that feeling of the sun hitting your face – and it suddenly feels like everything's going to be OK.' The good weather isn't taken for granted in Australia, with government grants offered to people with debilitating illnesses to spend time in the north of the country, where it's even warmer. 'Because there's still a sense that the sun is good for you,' says Ben, '– that we're lucky to have it. We call ourselves the "lucky country".'

'Lucky' is the word. Australians have a good welfare system with free healthcare and education up to University, after which there are zero-interest student loans to cover fees and living expenses. Many finish work at 5 p.m. and 85 per cent of Australians live within 50 km of the sea, so can toddle off to one of the country's 10,000 stunning beaches to surf every day if they want to. There's space to breathe, with only three Australians per square kilometre countrywide, and most Australians spend a lot of time outdoors.

'The weather makes you want to be outside and you don't want to do that by yourself, so it makes for a really good social environment,' says Sheridan. And friendship is really important to Australians. Ninety-four per cent of Aussies say that they know someone they could rely on in time of need, according to OECD data. 'We make strong connections with people in Australia, but it's quite "easy come",' Sheridan tells me, ' – so I'd be offended if someone didn't want to be my friend, it's like, "What's wrong with you?!"' This is fascinating, and the antithesis to the British or even Danish approach to friendship whereby you must either have been introduced formally by at least two family members or have been at school with someone for years. That or have met on Twitter. But Ben agrees that his fellow countrymen and women are unusually open to making new mates via face-to-face interaction.

'In Australia, you'll chat to your barista while they're making you coffee and they might say "Wanna go for a beer?"' *And you'll go?* I am near incredulous at such social confidence. 'Yes.' *And not just because they're a hot girl and you fancy them?* I've known Ben a month but this seems a fair punt. 'Yes...' he says, before qualifying: ' – seventy per cent of the time, "yes". But even then, we all tend to have a lot in common in Australia so you know you could always talk to them about sports or coffee or beaches...' Sheridan is similarly unabashed: 'We'll talk to anyone – hairdressers, baristas, store workers – you build up a personal relationship. If there's a connection, there's nothing weird about taking that further.' Liz only needs to sit next to someone on a bus and she'll become their lifelong friend (and they'll be all the better for it: she's a good one). Friendship, for Australians, is like 'no worries' – approached with generosity but no less sincere for being spread around liberally. It strikes me that this must be a rather lovely way to live – going through life assuming that everyone you meet is just waiting to be your friend. Between a friendly, laid-back attitude, a love of the outdoors, the sun, and a passionate belief in a 'fair go' for all, why wouldn't you be happy? So go forth: be fair, befriend, give everything a try. Remember: we're not here to fuck spiders.

HOW TO ADOPT A 'FAIR GO' APPROACH TO LIFE AND HARNESS A 'NO WORRIES' MENTALITY

1

Give everyone you meet a 'fair go', from potential new friends to the office intern who always breaks the printer – and your barista.

2

Give everything you do a 'fair crack'. Trying is not to be underestimated and enthusiasm is the most attractive human quality there is.

3

Remember your good fortune: we may not all live in the 'lucky country' but we've all got things we can be grateful for.

4

Pain of a day ahead of you? It'll be over this time tomorrow. No worries. Really. Because what's the point?

5

Sun's out = guns out. Or at least, your face. Post-application of SPF 50, obviously. Close your eyes, lift your chin to the sky, and experience the sensation of the warm sun hitting your skin. Suddenly, it feels like everything's going to be OK...

Gross National Happiness (GNH) is the philosophy that guides the government and people of Bhutan whereby collective happiness and well-being is measured and prioritised ahead of financial gain. Although practised informally throughout Bhutanese history, the term was coined in 1972 when King Jigme Singye Wangchuck told a journalist from *The Financial Times*, 'Gross National Happiness is more important than Gross National Product'. Since then, Bhutan has championed policies that measure 'prosperity' via the spiritual, physical, social and environmental health of its citizens and the natural environment.

BHUTAN

The air is sharp; the sky is wide and pierced by mountains – so high they disappear into clouds. And yet the tiny Himalayan nation of just 750,000 people, where cows still roam the streets, has been quietly changing the world.

Until 1962 Bhutan had no roads, schools, hospitals or national currency, but then the Third King, Jigme Dorji Wangchuck, known as 'the father of modern Bhutan', began to update the infrastructure before handing over the reins to his son. King Jigme Singye Wangchuck, the Fourth King, stepped into his father's *tshoglham* (traditional Bhutanese boots) in his teens and took on the mantle of propelling his country into the modern era – in a particularly Bhutanese way.

Bhutan already had a long tradition of promoting happiness, well-being and the importance of karma, having adopted Buddhism some time around AD 700. 'Compassion and altruism in Bhutan are as old as the mountains,' says Passang, a friend of a friend from Paro, the town with the only international airport in Bhutan. The term '*ga-kyid*' is essential to most Bhutanese – from *ga* for 'happiness' and *kyid* for 'peace' – but, as Passang says, 'the concept transcends the literal meaning to encompass spiritual, environmental, social and economic wellbeing.' Two ancient proverbs give a telling account of the priorities of the Bhutanese, historically: 'There is no way to happiness: happiness is the way', and

'Happiness is based on trust and trust is free'. As a result, Bhutan had been chugging along by itself quite nicely, albeit aided by the addition of such novelties as hospitals, schools, and roads by which to get to them.

When King Wangchuck IV came to power in 1972, he wanted to continue his father's work as a moderniser but wasn't so keen on some of the consumerist trappings and ensuing troubles that came with them in other countries he observed. He saw the direction the rest of the world was going in and he didn't like it. But, rather than isolating his kingdom from outside influences, he set out to eschew the relentless pursuit of cold hard cash at the cost of human well-being and promote *ga-kyid* – as well as finding a balance between the old and the new.

'In naming the GNH, King Wangchuck formalised the ideals and belief system that Bhutanese people had been operating under for years,' says Tsewang, a contact of mine originally from Thimphu, the capital of Bhutan: 'This ensured that the advantages of the old way of life were not lost with the encroachment of modern technology.' The country opened up to television and the internet at the end of the 1990s and even welcomed the delights of *WrestleMania*, Indian soap operas and Kit Kats ('very popular'), but the traditional ideas also endured. Then in 2005, at the height of his popularity, King Wangchuck IV abdicated to live out his own personal happiness dream in a tree house (apparently), and let his son, Jigme Khesar Namgyel Wangchuck, have a go. The new king, Wangchuck V, began his reign overseeing the democratisation of his country and in 2008 GNH was instituted as the official goal of the government in the Constitution of Bhutan – at the same time as the rest of the world was falling apart.

Amidst growing inequality, environmental Armageddon and banking crashes in every developed country going, Bhutan's alternative approach started getting some attention. In 2011, the then secretary-general of the UN, Ban Ki-moon, urged UN member nations to follow the example of Bhutan and measure happiness and well-being – calling happiness a 'fundamental human goal'. The following year, the UN's secretary-general met with Bhutan's prime minister Jigme Thinley to talk tactics and form a strategy to encourage the spread of Bhutan's GNH Index and improve levels of well-being worldwide. Because, here's the thing: it works.

Both healthcare and education are now free and universal in Bhutan – a result of being prioritised as part of the GNH programme. This has doubled life expectancy and 100 per cent of Bhutanese children are now enrolled in primary school. 'Children study Gross National Happiness at school and it's part of the mainstream agenda,' says Tsewang, '– but this isn't just an academic thing. It means a lot to your average person, too.' Every two years a study is run by a government think-tank asking everyone in Bhutan about their lives and happiness. A 'Gross National Happiness Commission' then measures happiness and well-being across nine 'key indicators' for a happy life, namely: psychological well-being, health, time use, education, cultural diversity and resilience, good governance, community vitality, living standards and ecological diversity. And ecology matters in Bhutan.

All commercial or governmental moves are screened through the prism of GNH to see what impact they'll have on the environment and society as a whole, regardless of financial gain. There is a clear link between sustainability and happiness, according to Happiness Research Institute data, and the

European Social Survey found that people who care for the environment report higher levels of subjective well-being. Being green certainly makes Tsewang happy – and it's something that new arrivals often comment on. 'Visitors remark that they've never seen such lush forests or such intact landscapes anywhere else in the world,' says Tsewang. '– but this is part of the GNH.' Bhutan is one of the only developing countries putting 'sustainability' at the heart of its political agenda and has pledged to remain carbon neutral and to ensure that at *least* 60 per cent of its landmass is covered by forest, forever (it's currently 70 per cent). The country is so luscious that Bengal tigers are fleeing India for Bhutan because their habitat's being demolished back home. Export logging has been banned and Bhutan discourages private vehicles from the roads with a monthly 'pedestrian day'. Tsewang tells me how Bhutan recently turned down an opportunity to join the World Trade Organization because membership would have necessitated opening up Bhutan's forests and other natural resources in a way that wasn't compatible with GNH goals for the environment. Bhutan also made its excuses to McDonald's and their cash to protect Bhutanese waistlines. 'We do still have Kit Kats though,' he admits, although the Bhutanese government is currently trying to reduce unhealthy imports and encourage healthy eating habits with the goal of an 'organic 2020'.

'It's a *process*,' Tsewang tells me. 'People need to go through some unhealthy cycles to see and feel it for themselves. Because being told what to do won't make everyone happy.' And GNH is about happiness for everyone. 'We're not an individualistic society,' says Tsewang. 'Everything is done together in Bhutan and we don't prioritise privacy like some cultures do. There is no "privacy" in Bhutan!' But the flipside of this is that there's also little loneliness. 'You might have twenty people sharing a room and then there'll be another twenty all sitting down to breakfast together,' says Tsewang, professing: 'I love it this way – this is how we share our limited resources and there's a real sense of community. Sharing is love.'

Bhutan isn't paradise and everyday life is hard for many, with physically demanding work in harsh environments. Men and women still have markedly different roles in Bhutanese society and in the highlands, nomads still practise polygamy with multiple wives to help cart children about and tend cattle. Which isn't my idea of fun.

The advent of modernity hasn't been without its challenges, either. Technology has been a disruption, admits Tsewang, with television arriving in the 1990s (see *WrestleMania*) and a few of Bhutan's sixty or so different dialects from fragmented communities starting to die out in favour of English or Dzongkha (the national language). But technologies like WeChat (the Chinese messaging and social media app) have also helped revive some dialects, with groups set up online to share learnings. And those without reading or writing skills in some communities are now able to talk to each other via video chats. Bhutan's education minister and prime minister have encouraged STEM subjects in schools [science, technology, engineering, mathematics] and children are learning to build their own computers and drones. 'We've even got our own MIT lab,' adds Tsewang with pride.

The GNH aims to honour the best bits of traditional Bhutanese culture, too. 'If you get sick, you can opt to be treated in the traditional Bhutanese medicine system or the conventional medicine system – even in hospital,' Tsewang tells me. Whereas Western medicine treats only the sickness, the traditional Bhutanese medicine system treats the human as whole, ' – so it's good to have both,' is how Tsewang and many Bhutanese people see it. It isn't always easy to combine old and new. 'We're a country at a crossroads, where ancient minds and modern minds are meeting,' says Tsewang. 'We need to reflect on where we've come from and where we're going. And we have to have compassion for our fellow human beings.' Passang mentioned compassion, too, and I'm interested in whether this is part of GNH. Tsewang assures me it's integral. 'GNH actively promotes compassion – that's all part of it,' he says – and because none of us know what's happening in someone else's life, 'we all need to elevate our compassion.'

There's nothing smug about the GNH, the way Tsewang and Passang describe it to me: the Bhutanese aren't claiming to be happy; they're saying that they're committed to working on it. 'Buddhism dictates that we're all on a journey in this lifetime, and that whatever action we take here and now – good or bad – will impact on our future in this life, as well as the next when we are reincarnated,' says Passang. He tells me how most Bhutanese will assume that someone living a stress-free life with plenty of good fortune is being rewarded for their deeds in their previous life – and vice versa. Because: karma. 'If you steal or lie and if you have expensive lawyers you can probably get away with it in conventional law,' says Tsewang, 'but you'll never get peace from karma.'

This makes the karmic system both simpler and more advanced than any conventional approach. Karma also reminds people that their current incarnation is fleeting. 'You see a lot of death and suffering in Bhutan but you become reconciled to it,' says Passang. This takes away its sting. No one fears death in Bhutan and cremation grounds are located centrally in communities as a reminder to reflect on the impermanence of this life. 'If someone's died, you'll know from kilometres away,' says Tsewang. 'You'll see the smoke coming out of the furnace and children will point it out to each other – so the circle of karma is always in the Bhutanese consciousness.' Worshippers at temples in Bhutan are also encouraged to prostrate themselves and 'park their ego' in order to let learning and inspiration in.

The terrain keeps locals humble, too, with huge mountains dwarfing mere mortals and maintaining the sense that we as humans are insignificant – a small part of a whole, unpredictable world filled with numerous species. 'Our ultimate goal is to co-exist with nature,' says Tsewang. 'We believe that all the animals are our brothers, sisters, children or parents in another lifetime, so we take care of them.' There's a saying in Bhutan that 'we don't inherit this planet from forefathers, we borrow it from our children.' A remarkable way of looking at the world – and a lesson for us all.

HOW TO LIVE ACCORDING TO GNH

1

Elevate your compassion: next time you feel frustrated with a colleague
or ready to throw a sock at a loved one who has failed to put
his underwear in the laundry basket, just for example...
('IN the basket: not around it. IN it!') consider that they've got their own
things going on and probably don't mean to wind you up.

2

Park your ego. What would happen if you assumed nothing and
let in life lessons from everyone and everything you encountered?
Has your dog/bus conductor/frustrating colleague been trying to
tell you something, all this time...?

3

Live sustainably wherever possible. Look after the natural world and look
after yourself, today – so that both have a fighting chance of a tomorrow.

4

Prioritise happiness over money. Researchers from San Francisco State
University have proven that we get far more joy from experiences than
from accumulating and buying more 'stuff' that we don't need anyway.

5

Remember: there is no way to happiness, happiness is the way.
The journey is it, so travel well.

SAUDADE

*S*audade (pronounced '*sow-DAH-djee*'), noun, a feeling of longing, melancholy, or nostalgia for a happiness that once was – or even a happiness that you merely hoped for. First recorded in the 13th-century poetry collection, the *Cancioneiro da Ajuda, saudade* was popularised in the 15th century when Portuguese ships sailed to Africa and Asia and those left behind felt the loss of loved ones who had departed. The Portuguese colonised Brazil in the 16th century and the word was taken up by those who settled there to remember the homeland they'd left behind. Now considered characteristic of both the Portuguese and Brazilian temperament.

BRAZIL

Brazil, the country of carnival, football and nuts, also has a word for the absence of happiness – a term of such beauty that it bestows a perverse joy on its users. *Saudade* represents a feeling so fundamental to the human experience that it warrants inclusion in this book, because, as the philosopher Kierkegaard wrote, there is 'bliss in melancholy and sadness'. Scientists over the years have concurred with Kierkegaard and researchers from the University of New South Wales found that sadness can help improve attention to detail, increase perseverance, and promote generosity. Most of us will have experienced a bittersweet pleasure in moments of melancholy – reminiscing, flicking through old photographs, or caring about anything or anyone enough to miss them when they're gone. The only way to avoid sadness and regret completely is by avoiding *life* – and we only appreciate the light if we've experienced shade. This is why *saudade* matters.

Originally associated with both the rise and fall of the Portuguese empire, saudade started life as an expression of sorrow felt for those who departed for long journeys, with survivors feeling that something was missing in their lives thereafter. But *saudade*'s ascendance in Brazil is from the perspective of the people newly arrived in a strange land – often against their will – rather than those left behind. The Portuguese made themselves so at home in Brazil that it's the only country in South America that speaks Portuguese. In other words, there's a whole lot of *saudade* going on.

Saudade often carries a sense that the thing you're nostalgic for won't ever happen again. As the 17th-century Portuguese writer Manuel de Melo put it, *saudade* is 'a pleasure you suffer, an ailment you enjoy'. It's inspired numerous artists over the years and a wealth of classical images of *saudade* show a father looking out to sea without knowing if his son will ever come back, or a widow wearing black because her love's been lost in a shipwreck, or children growing up fatherless because their dad's been deported. You know, the usual cheerful fare.

'It's a longing for someone or something that you don't have any more that you love – be it food, or weather, or a place you've lived or a person,' Danielle, originally from Fortaleza in the north-east, tells me. Today, there is an affectionate rivalry as to whether Brazil or Portugal 'own' *saudade*, but in terms of scale and suffering, Brazil wins. The majority of the Brazilian population was formed by the influx of Portuguese settlers and African slaves, mostly Bantu and West African people, so Brazil's history is messy and painful. Even once slavery had been outlawed in the 19th century, economic necessity forced many to leave their homes and the people they loved.

Throughout hundreds of years of deprivation, *saudade* became so central to the Brazilian psyche that it was given its own official 'day'. *Dia da Saudade* takes place on 30 January every year, when it's common to

hear music about nostalgia as well as to share poems and stories about the feeling and the people or places that have inspired it.

'It's "I love you"; it's "I miss you" – but *bigger*, it's everything,' says Danielle. '*Saudade* for me is the lingering memory of someone or something that you're really happy was a part of you. You may be sad because you haven't got it, but you remember it happily because you had it once.' *Saudade* can also describe the feeling of missing something that still exists, but that you can't have any more – like Opal Fruits or 'the one that got away'. Imagine if you'd ended up with your first love. Imagine a life with them. Strange, isn't it? A little like a 'Schrödinger's spouse', the relationship *might* have worked, but then again it might not. That heady, intoxicating, all-consuming lust, where you ache for someone and feel like you're falling out of a window, could never have lasted. Could it? If you found them again now, there might not be the spark that there once was. They might not be the same person any more. You certainly aren't. It *might* have been for the best that you lost each other when you did. Similarly, the widow at the docks in all the old *saudade* paintings could suddenly find out that her husband had survived, and he could come back a changed man, or having met

someone else. The sailor may return home, but his beloved might have moved on, his ailing parents might have died, his town might be different, he might end up feeling that he's lost connection with the very things he was nostalgic for just days before while at sea. There's an ambiguity in *saudade* – or, rather, a complexity – and an understanding that some losses are unavoidable, and that that's OK.

Psychologists agree that there is merit to this way of thinking. Acknowledging that sadness is part of our reality and that it's 'OK not to be OK' is healthy; it helps us to come to terms with the fact that some degree of suffering in life is normal and that we'll get through it. This doesn't mean that we care any less – we can mourn and experience full-blown *saudade*, then get on with our day. With *saudade*, we can have our emotional cake and eat it too – no wonder it's been a muse for so many artists over the years. Musicians, too, have taken their cue from *saudade* and it's inspired bossa nova composers from João Gilberto to Vinicius de Moraes and Tom Jobim, who wrote the now famous 'Chega de Saudade'. This song has a very special place in Danielle's heart, she tells me, because: 'My husband played it to me when he was trying to get me to go out with him.' It worked: she's currently seven months pregnant. 'It's melancholy,' she tells me as we listen to the song on YouTube, '– but it's a pleasant melancholy. And it's a counterbalance to that very "up", sometimes over the top, Brazilian carnival spirit.'

Saudade has been described as a 'presence of absence' – a bit like desire – and 'you can be among thousands of people but none is the one you want to be by your side,' is how Danielle puts it. But it's not a pity party: '*Saudade* is the moment you realise how important people are in your life and the moments you've taken for granted,' she says. So *saudade* makes you grateful for what you've got – and aware it might be gone in a heartbeat. This is an approach to happiness that's been around for millennia, with the Stoic philosopher Seneca recommending that we imagine losing everything – regularly – so we learn to value what we have. And yet somehow, in the rest of the world, we've forgotten this useful lesson. Negative emotions and thoughts – even ones that might ultimately be helpful – tend to get pushed down and buried under a fug of 'busy' or 'just haven't had enough coffee yet this morning'. But not in Portugal or Brazil. '*Saudade* makes us feel things more deeply,' says Danielle, '– both the sadness and the joy. And it reminds us to celebrate what we have. So we're always ready to dance; we're always ready to love; and we're always ready to welcome in loved ones.'

Hospitality is next to holiness in Brazil and Danielle tells me she has relatives who vacuum twice a day in case visitors come around. 'You see your friends every week. At *least*. And then I have about a million cousins...' she tells me, 'so we always have extra food so that we can invite them to join us for whatever the next meal may be.' The first question a Brazilian will ask when they open the door to someone is often 'Have you eaten?' and in the country of carnival it's little surprise that there's a warmth to the national character. The climate helps: it's 30 degrees most of the year where Danielle is from, 'except in winter when it's 27 degrees...' she says. But they're also a tactile bunch. Another of my favourite Portuguese words is *cafuné* – the act of someone touching your hair or head in a loving, caressing way, like a massage ('we're big fans of *cafuné* in Brazil') and *aconchego* or 'warmth' – meaning to be held or welcomed by someone. 'We're always touching. We're always demonstrative,' says

Danielle, hugging herself as she speaks. Human touch releases oxytocin, the 'love hormone', which promotes feelings of well-being and is the best cure for loneliness, according to neuroscientists. But there's something else, too, says Danielle: 'We're also more open to joy than you probably find in the rest of the world.' Indeed, there's even the carnival-esque word *desbundar*, meaning 'shedding your inhibitions and having fun'.

Carnival season kicks off in January and Rio is the biggest of the bunch, 'but really it's everywhere,' Danielle tells me, adding that people dance in the streets in broad daylight. Sober? 'Mostly!' *Wow*. Dancing not only releases endorphins (in common with exercise in general) but studies from the University of Hertfordshire have shown that it also improves self-esteem. 'In Brazil, we get a catharsis from really letting our hair down like this. We're more relaxed,' Danielle tells me, 'and it's the same with *saudade*. It's a way to cope – a way to survive when there are so many problems for many people – like with the government for example.' Political corruption is widespread in Brazil. 'People also work long hours; there's huge social inequality and high unemployment rates – so we learn early on to be happy with less,' Danielle tells me. Seeing family and friends, whenever she can, is what's most important. And remembering

them when they're not around any more is a way of honouring them, as well as 'exhaling' our emotions – good and bad.

I like the idea of celebrating happiness past as well as present. *Saudade* feels like a love letter to loss: a necessary slackening to stay afloat and a way to acknowledge the people we care for as well as our hopes and dreams – whether they'd have turned out the way we envisage or not. I miss my grandfather. I miss an old friend who I can never be as close to as I'd like to be again. I ache for both. But I'm grateful that they were in my life for the time they were. And now I'd quite like to go and have a cry for them. And then, maybe, I'll feel like dancing...

HOW TO EXPERIENCE *SAUDADE*

1

Listen to 'Chega de Saudade' to get you in the mood. Search for it on vinyl for extra melancholic nostalgia.

2

Look back at old photographs on Facebook of that friend you've lost touch with, or the ex you still think fondly of and can't help wishing was still in your life. Instead of blocking out the feelings that ensue, surrender to the longing and reminisce.

3

Spend time remembering those you've loved and lost – then practise being a little more grateful for the ones who are still around.

4

Give yourself a whole day to celebrate *saudade* – the Brazilians do it on 30 January but you can choose whenever suits you. Watch old movies, listen to music that makes you remember times past, dig out your old love letters (millennials: emails or texts will do).

JOIE DE VIVRE

Joie de vivre – or 'joy of living' in its English translation – is a phrase used to express an enthusiastic, buoyant enjoyment of life. In use in France since the late 17th century, the term was chronicled by Émile Zola in his 1883 novel, *La Joie de vivre*. Since then, *joie de vivre* has evolved into something approaching a secular religion in the French-speaking world but it's the Canadians who have taken the idea most to heart to describe their national temperament.

CANADA

O Canada! Country of moose, maple syrup, my mother-in-law and Justin Trudeau: we salute you. Not just for your bears, beavers, mounted police and my mother-in-law (though, obviously, them...) but for your unassailable *joie de vivre*. A country of 36 million people spread across 9 million square kilometres, America's more socially liberal neighbour has space on its side, as well as a reputation for 'nice'. What's more, Canada has been ranked in the top ten happiest nations since the UN World Happiness Report was first published in 2012, thanks to a generous dollop of *joie de vivre*.

'We have happiness in all aspects of life here,' says Mélanie, a friend of a friend from Montreal. 'We have good food, good friends, good seasons – and *joie de vivre* is the most commonly used term to describe happiness in Canada.' *Joie de vivre* is especially prevalent in Quebec, the French-speaking province that is officially the happiest place in the

country, according to a study published in the *Canadian Public Policy* journal. Quebeckers are so happy that were Quebec a nation unto itself, it would be second only to Denmark in international life-satisfaction rankings. 'It's because we're French,' Mélanie tells me, 'but you know, we're not *France* French.' And this is an important distinction.

Full disclosure: most of the *France*-French people I know – despite being wonderful in their ways – aren't much like the film *Amélie*. In fact the only French person I've ever met who's like the film *Amélie* is actually called Amélie and describes herself as 'the least French French person ever'. Despite being a huge Francophile and having worked or holidayed in France every year, forever, I can't help finding the outlook of many Serge

Gainsbourg-alikes somewhat downbeat (what other nation would describe an orgasm as 'a little death'?). It's as though, as one Canadian friend puts it, 'Quebec is full of the French who were too happy for France...' So when it comes to *joie de vivre*, Canada triumphs (*pardonnez-moi*).

The first clue as to 'why' comes courtesy of Canada's infrastructure. High taxes re-distribute wealth to reduce inequality and fund free healthcare, great education – and a social safety net to catch you if you fall. Religious tolerance is widespread and Canada was the first country outside Europe to legalise same-sex marriage. It's good for women, with decent parental leave and Justin Trudeau famously naming a gender-balanced cabinet when he came to power, 'Because it's 2015'.

'It's also a really safe place to live,' says Mélanie. 'We have low crime rates and strict gun control so we know we're not going to get shot going about our business here.' For many, this may seem immaterial – an attribute to be taken for granted. But living near America, the absence of firearms in your average home is a distinct plus. 'We're not afraid in Canada,' says Mélanie, '– and this means we can enjoy life more.' Brad, a colleague of a friend from Montreal, agrees: 'I can walk around anywhere at 3 a.m. without fear – and I can't remember the last time I saw someone lose their temper. Confrontations and public displays of anger are almost unheard of.'

Diversity is key and Canada has

long placed an emphasis on inclusiveness. In 2015 Justin Trudeau went to the airport to personally greet Syrian refugees and help hand out warm winter coats (I love him. Can you tell?). Multiculturalism is regularly cited as one of Canada's biggest achievements and the ability to celebrate difference is a distinguishing feature of Canadian identity. 'We're less individualistic than in the US,' says Mélanie, 'and togetherness is important to us, so we want everyone to feel welcome.' Researchers from Montreal's McGill University found that people who feel part of a common society tend to do well on life-satisfaction surveys. Unlike the 'melting pot' model, ethnic groups in Canada are encouraged to keep their own identities. 'We're a "cultural mosaic",' says Mélanie, 'and being part of a diverse society is a really positive thing for most Canadians, something that contributes to our *joie de vivre*.'

Ottawa-born philosopher John Ralston Saul has described Canada as a 'soft' country with a flexible identity, as opposed to the brittle, patriarchal identities of other states (oh hi, USA!). He argues that the Canadian mindset has been heavily influenced by First Nation ideas of equality as well as a preference for negotiation over violence (thus the aversion to conflict). Instead of crushing Aboriginal values, Canada largely embraced them. There are still challenges – and, as Canadian

Avril Lavigne sings, it's 'complicated'. Trudeau has been criticised for approving oil pipelines through First Nations land and fisheries, although many First Nations have approved the pipelines. Today there are 634 recognised First Nations governments spread across Canada and the country is one of the world's most ethnically diverse and multicultural nations, thanks to large-scale immigration. 'Most Canadians see this as A Good Thing,' says Mélanie, 'because we all benefit from diversity of ideas and opinions.' It makes sense from a business viewpoint, too – and Canada swerved the full force of the 2008 financial crisis because its diversified banking system made it more robust.

'A big difference in Canada compared to the rest of the world is people's willingness to help if something does go wrong,' says Brad, explaining that a strong sense of community mixed with individualism allows for high levels of trust, 'without compromising privacy'. So Canadians will hold open the door for you; offer help if you look lost; and lend a hand if you need it – all while maintaining a cheery ebullience. They're also teeth-tinglingly polite. My husband has told one of our Canadian friends the same story every time they've met for the past year. Our kids go to the same kindergarten, we live ten minutes away, and his wife and I share an appreciation for cava and learning to paddle board (badly). Ergo, we meet fairly frequently. Yet Mr Canada is so polite he has never once stopped my husband in his tracks and yelled: 'Enough already! I know all a-boot the time it got so cold the fjord froze! You tell me every time I see you! Which, considering our kids go to the same kindergarten, we live ten minutes away, and your wife and mine share an appreciation for cava and learning to paddle board (badly) is fairly frequently!' Instead, he smiles, raises his eyebrows semi-convincingly, and says something appropriately upbeat about that story being 'Amazing!' Every. Single. Time.

'We're pretty respectful,' says Mélanie, 'so we probably wouldn't call you out on something small, preferring to just get on and have a good time instead.' Noted. And 'having a good time' is something people from Quebec do well. 'You can always tell Quebeckers at a corporate dinner, as their voices will rise as they drink,' says Mélanie.'It's the European in us, I guess! We definitely know how to enjoy life.' Researchers surveying the differences between Quebeckers and other Canadians found that *joie de vivre* was the top rated value in Quebec, but ranked fourth in the rest of Canada, according to Leger data (the largest Canadian-owned polling and research organisation). 'We like a party and we get a lot of pleasure out of being together,' says Mélanie. 'We go out a lot – even when we have kids or a busy job, we make the most of the amazing variety of restaurants and cuisines around us and go to festivals in summer.' Montreal is known as the City of Festivals, with more than eighty of these a year ranging from comedy to jazz, fireworks, flowers and film. Attending communal events and regular, diarised celebrations boosts well-being and promotes a sense of belonging, both of which play strongly into the Canadian idea of happiness and *joie de vivre*.

'We're outdoorsy, too,' says Mélanie, 'and the four distinct seasons provide us with a variety of activities, like skiing and hiking and biking. This makes for a healthy, happy, life.' As well as releasing endorphins, being active out of doors is good for our mental health according to Harvard research. And appreciating the natural world around us is a prime example of *joie de vivre*.

There are some sporting institutions guaranteed to get a Canadian's heart rate going and nothing gets them giddier than a good puck. Ice hockey was developed in Montreal, where the first indoor game was played in 1875 – and Canadians have never looked back. 'We do love our hockey,' admits Mélanie when I ask about this national stereotype, and there's such fervour for the sport that flights are sometimes delayed until the end of an important game because passengers won't board until they've found out who's won on TV. This serves as a bonding tool, providing essential water-cooler chat, no matter which team you support – and just mentioning the H-word is enough to bring a grin to most Canadians' faces. The other national obsession that can be loosely termed as 'sporting' is canoe-sex. 'A Canadian is someone who knows how

to make "it" in a canoe', is a quote attributed to the late Canadian writer and social commentator Pierre Berton. Although there are zero statistics on how many Canadians have actually had sex in a boat, it apparently tops the bucket list for many. So Canadians are closet thrill-seekers who are also polite, inclusive, and have Justin Trudeau. I know: it's too much.

Living in Quebec makes Brad 'extremely happy' and he tells me he has no plans to move out of his Canadian 'haven' anytime soon. Brad is a man who knows what he wants from life: he works hard, plays hard, and has an email sign-off the rest of us work-life wannabes need to adopt immediately. It reads:

Cheers, Brad
*Please note that I check my email at 12:30 p.m. and 6:00 p.m.
on weekdays only*

We all need to be more Brad. As well as being nicer to each other, being more active and prioritising fun with loved ones more often. 'They're simple things but they make us happier,' says Mélanie, 'and a positive, inclusive mindset is what *joie de vivre* is all about.' None of us knows what will happen when we die, so we should all try to take joy from the 'living' part as much as we can. Now.

HOW TO BE MORE CANADIAN AND FIND YOUR *JOIE DE VIVRE*

1

Be more polite, please. Thank you.

2

...But be firm when it comes to work life balance (and change your email sign-off pronto).

3

Get outdoors and use your body. Remind yourself of how amazing humans are and how wonderful the natural world really is.

4

Fill up your calendar – strong ties with family, friends and co-workers are part of what keeps Canadians happy.

5

Open up your social circle to welcome in new people and celebrate diversity – we're all richer from a plurality of voices.

6

Still need a pick-me-up? Google 'Justin Trudeau election campaign ad' where he gamely pokes fun at his own 'Canadian political hair' (or my personal 'Break in Case of Emergency', 'Justin Trudeau tattoo' *no, YOU'RE blushing...*)

XINGFU

Xingfu (pronounced *'zing-fu'*), noun, meaning 'the state of being happy' from *xin*, the Mandarin for 'lucky', and *fu* – meaning to have enough or just what you need in life. Unlike the English translation of happiness, *xingfu* refers not to a good mood, but a good life that is sufficient, sustainable, and has meaning. The term originated during the Han Dynasty – the second imperial dynasty of China dating from 206 BC to AD 220.

CHINA

Wei sets down his brush, pushes his glasses up his nose, and stands back to survey his work: a series of thick, black lines painted with the utmost control and precision on reams of white paper. This contemporary Chinese calligraphy, or 'line work' as Wei calls it, is beautiful and meditative all at once. And making it is Wei's *xingfu*.

'*Xingfu* is meaning, or purpose – it's a deeper sense of the word "happy",' Wei explains, pressing a palm to his chest and magically managing to avoid getting paint on his mandarin-collared black shirt. While many cultures have happiness terms that are to do with pleasure or short-term feelings, *xingfu* is the 'status of your life', as Wei puts it. We meet one wet Monday in an old spinning mill that's now a work space for creative types in my town and Wei tells me how his own *xingfu* meant swapping China for design school in Denmark, where he now lives and works. 'I wanted creative fulfilment from my career and I felt there was some part of me missing in China.' So he chose *Denmark*? With all the taxes? He smiles: '*Xingfu* can't be fulfilled by material things.' Lucky, that. 'Of course, *xingfu* requires some money – enough to buy food and pay for shelter. Plus I have to buy paint,' he gestures to the metal buckets filled with a glossy black lacquer that I'm terrified of tripping over: 'But this was the place where I could live my *meaning*.' Studies show that having a sense of purpose can make us happier and researchers at University College London found that having a sense of meaning might also increase our lifespan.

Xingfu is an ancient concept, denoting a set of value systems that are uniquely Chinese. To understand the term in its original Mandarin – 幸福 – I seek out the expertise of John, the colleague of a friend from Shenzhen. John practises traditional Chinese calligraphy and is (a) kind and (b) patient, deigning to explain in layperson's terms the building blocks of *xingfu*'s Mandarin characters. 'Basically,' he tells me, 'it's torture.'

All right, John, take it easy!

We all feel like that sometimes... But John means this literally: 'The character for *xing* [幸] represents torture, or some kind of penalty – a device that would be placed on the head, or your neck, or a foot.' *Good times*. 'The inference here is that if an emperor or powerful person gave you a pardon – an exemption from this torture – you would be lucky. 'Hence, *xing* or 幸 in modern Mandarin means "luck".'

The symbol for *fu* – 福 – is made up of three images: 'On the left there is some clothing,' says John, 'then the picture on the top right is of a mouth, so this represents food. The graphic beneath this is a grid of fields representing farmland. So *fu* implies that as long as you have sufficient food, clothing and farmland, you'll be OK.' And this is paired with a character that implies you're lucky if you escape torture...? 'Exactly!' John looks pleased that I may be finally 'getting it': 'So *xingfu* is having what you need or the essentials for life, plus some luck – because some things are beyond your control,' says John.

This is the 'long view' on happiness – sometimes things will be going well and sometimes they won't, but it's how they work out overall that matters. The notion of long-term happiness is in contrast to other Mandarin words such as *kāixīn* or *kuàilè*, which refer to states of fleeting happiness or short-lived highs. *Xingfu* = less of a rollercoaster, more of an eighty-year slog, if we're lucky (or *xing*). And although we can think about what our own *xingfu* might be, we can never chase it as such. 'You can't pursue *xingfu*, because it's not only an external thing,' Wei explains. So while *xingfu* necessitates a basic level of money to subsist (and buy paint) as well as good relationships with others, there are also variables – like desire. 'People might already have achieved their "goals" but still they don't feel they are living a *xingfu* life because their desires grow bigger and bigger,' says Wei. Or, as John puts it: 'Happiness is the things you possess divided by the things you expect.'

Let's all take a moment to plan where we will have this tattooed on our body and/or commission a bespoke slogan T-shirt. Whatever your inking proclivity, John speaks sense: if you're a millionaire but you want to be a billionaire, you won't be happy. Your *xingfu* consists of reasonable material possessions plus realistic expectations, not too high and not too low. This is why *xingfu* must be approached from the 'inside out', appreciating what we already have internally.

Your *xingfu* was relatively simple historically, since over a basic level of income your necessities were taken care of and you had some leisure time with which to think, feel and contemplate life's meaning. 'Typical Chinese parents wanted you to eat well, aspire to a stable job, a good marriage, children, and a house. That was it. That was enough,' says Wei. There were three traditional influences on Chinese values and ideas of happiness, he tells me: Confucianism, Taoism and Buddhism.

Confucius (551–479 BC) was the Chinese teacher, politician and philosopher who emphasised humanism, the cultivation of knowledge, and the idea that everyone should follow a path designed to enhance the greater good. Taoism, by contrast, emphasises simplicity and the importance of the natural order of things, as well Yin and Yang – a way

of seeing the world as a series of opposing yet complementary forces. And then there's Buddhism, the path to follow Buddha's teaching to 'end the suffering of reincarnation and gain the wisdom of seeing the real truth of life', as Wei puts it. I tell Wei that this is quite the metaphysical cocktail to be growing up with and he nods gravely and looks suddenly tired, as if all the weight of the ancients were upon him. Then he adjusts his glasses and says: 'At least, this is how it was historically.' Because times have changed.

'With the fall of traditional China and the rise of new China, a lot of people want to be "the best",' says Wei, '– always needing "more".' This isn't doing wonders for their *xingfu*. 'There were a lot of good traditional values in China but the Cultural Revolution killed all the old stuff,' says Wei. Casualties were famously catastrophic and it's estimated that 30 million people died. 'Some things weren't great before the revolution,' says Wei, 'but aside from the lives lost, people are starting to realise we lost some important values, too, and *xingfu* is at risk for many in modern China.' Whenever Wei goes back to his hometown, five hours' north of Beijing, he sees friends who are so busy working to get 'more' of everything that they don't stop to think about what will fulfil them. 'They don't think about their purpose,' he says. Dramatic inflation, especially in property prices, means that the aspiration to have a house that Wei's parents would have viewed as a perfectly normal basic necessity – part of their *xingfu* – is now out of reach for many (as in other capital cities). 'In Beijing it's very expensive to buy a house,' says Wei, 'so you could spend your whole life trying.' But there is hope.

It's now so hard to get on the property ladder for many that they are beginning to return to a simpler way of life. 'It's happening slowly, but China is becoming more open to new ideas,' he says. 'Young people are travelling, seeing what the rest of the world is like, and witnessing a different way of life.' This is a positive thing in Wei's eyes: 'The balance might swing back and younger Chinese people might reclaim the traditional values as well as their *xingfu*.' Yolanda from Shanghai tells me how she grew up with the idea that to have 'a good life', she had to be a grade-A student in the hope of getting 'a decent job', getting a house, acquiring a family, and so 'being happy', but for her son, things are different. 'Whereas we all wanted to fit in, young people these days want to have their own character and be different,' she says: 'They don't want to follow their parents' or their teachers' instructions and are more eager to challenge and speak out.' This means that the next generation are better equipped to pursue their *xingfu*, regardless of their parents' or society's expectations. Millennials could be the least materialistic generation yet, saving us all by scrolling through Instagram and Snapchat and seeing how the other billion live. Snowflakes = our saviours. Perhaps...

Back in Wei's studio, we both stare at his latest creation – a vast, broad-brushed expression of curves followed by angular dashes, all in a continuous line that somehow brings to mind a feeling of harmony. I ask him what it means. He asks, 'What do you think it means?' I hate that. I tell him I like my art with labels and he tells me he doesn't do labels. Yeah: Wei is *that* Zen. But I also feel strangely soothed after talking to him and getting an introduction to *xingfu*. After a day in which I've dealt with vomiting offspring, had a row with my husband over coffee (actually about coffee, rather than just whilst consuming a tasty beverage) and smashed the screen of my iPhone (doubtless made in Shenzhen to start with) I feel surprisingly positive. And now I'm looking at a series of shapes and patterns that I don't understand in a literal sense but that make me feel as close to serene as I'm possibly ever going to be capable of. Almost as though some of Wei's preternatural calm is being offered back to me in his work. I prepare to say goodbye and Wei shares with me a little of the wisdom of the Buddha: 'We have to be happy with what we already have. We have to be generous, compassionate, tolerant and spiritual, to find our meaning and so our happiness. That's *xingfu*.' And I finally exhale.

HOW TO EXPERIENCE *XINGFU*

1

Make like Wei and paint. Or draw. Or take up gardening.
Do something where you can feel or experience without intellectualising.
The left side of our brain is responsible for performing tasks that have to
do with logic, while the right side looks after creativity and the arts – so
give your left brain a rest for the night.

2

Find your inner Tibetan monk and go up high to get some peace,
perspective and just 'be' for a while.

3

Once you're ready to switch your left brain on again, think about what
you want. Not the *things* you want, but the *life* you want. Now write
down the steps needed to begin your journey. Your *xingfu*.

PURA VIDA

Pura vida, a phrase meaning 'pure life' that refers to staying optimistic and happy in spite of any negative circumstances around you. A term that defines Costa Rica and 'los ticos' (Costa Ricans). It can be used as a greeting ('Hi! Are you having *pura vida*?'); a farewell ('Happy to have seen you, *pura vida*!'); an expression of appreciation ('that was *pura vida*!'), as well as a mantra to live by. The phrase was introduced by the 1956 Mexican film of the same name and when it debuted in Costa Rica, '*pura vida*!' was taken up as the country's unofficial motto.

COSTA RICA

The sea is so still it seems like a mirror. The sunsets look as though they've been painted on. White sand shimmers with tiny crabs, so small they fit on your fingertips, and flowers of all colours share their scent on the warm summer breeze. This is Costa Rica. And this is *pura vida*. 'It's the place, it's the view, it's the state of mind: it's pure happiness,' says Ana, a friend from San José who now lives near me in Denmark. Ana is currently having a crappy time of it (technical term...) but her eyes light up as she talks about her homeland. '*Pura vida* means "everything's good",' she tells me, going on to describe her last trip back when the sun was always shining and she felt as though she had all the time in the world to enjoy it. She tells me about mornings spent on the beach drinking insanely good coffee before forest hikes in the afternoon, spotting monkeys, macaws, tapirs and tree frogs. I decide we should all move to Costa Rica, immediately. Or at the very least plan an *Atlas of Happiness* fieldtrip. But there's more: I learn that the Central American country is also home to the greatest density of species *in the world*, with over 500,000 unique specimens of plant and wildlife – and that the government has pledged to increase this number by dedicating a quarter of the country to conservation. Costa Ricans are so eco-woke that they've been able to produce 99 per cent of their electricity from renewable sources since 2015.

'We're also pretty healthy,' says Ana. I tell her that now she's just showing off, then wonder whether I can get her family to adopt me. 'There's so much fresh food and we're outside all of the time, so everyone swims or surfs or hikes – we're very active,' she tells me. Thanks to all this clean living and exercise, Costa Ricans enjoy higher levels of well-being than many of the wealthiest countries in the world. *Ticos* are said to be in the 'blue zone' – an anthropological concept that describes the regions of the world with the longest life expectancy, and the characteristic lifestyles and the environments of the people who live there. Extra kale for the Costa Ricans... 'But really, we do it because if you're healthier and you're taking care of yourself, you're happier, too,' says Ana.'That's *pura vida.*'

They're also pretty smart. Education is prioritised and since 1869 schooling has been free and mandatory. The country invests more in education and health as a proportion of its Gross Domestic Product than most other OECD countries – including the UK. Lifelong learning has been linked to better health and even a better social life, according to the *Harvard Business Review*, and if there's one thing Costa Ricans take seriously it's their social life. Close family connections and friends we see regularly are one of the key indicators for happiness in any given index, and *pura vida* mandates that you're out with your mates All The Time.

'There is a life, for everyone, outside of work,' says Ana. 'No matter who you are, seeing loved ones is very important to Costa Ricans.' Sunday is 'Grandma day', where everyone visits the matriarch of the family ('whether you like them or not!') and anyone who doesn't have biological family nearby makes a family unit of their own from friends. 'Friends are the family we choose,' says Ana, 'and we're really friendly in Costa Rica,' she tells me, explaining that if a *tico* meets you once, they'll talk to you and be 'really nice'. 'Then if they meet you a second time, we'll be hugging and making plans and talking, really going deep,' she says. 'From then on in, we're pretty much friends for life.'

Ana tells me how on her last trip 'home' a couple of weeks ago, she sent a message to one of her old teachers, not knowing if she'd get an answer or not but keen to reach out (because teachers = revered in Costa Rica). 'I'd always liked her, but we hadn't been in touch in twenty-five years,' Ana tells me. 'But my old teacher remembered me and said, '"Oh we

must meet up!"' So they did. And they ended up having dinner. And then she invited Ana to her birthday party the following day and insisted that the next time Ana passed through town, she should stay with her. 'This isn't unusual, either,' says Ana. 'We form bonds in Costa Rica – it doesn't matter how long I haven't seen you for, if I like you, I'll open my house to you.'

Pura vida necessitates opening your heart a little more than many northern Europeans might be accustomed to. 'It means "we love you and we're on your side, no matter what",' says Ana, so *ticos* can end up with an extended family of non-blood relations who will stick by them through thick and thin. 'That's a pretty nice feeling – to know you have a lot of friends like that who'd do anything for you,' Ana tells me, and I believe her. 'It's the Latin American character,' she explains. 'We have passionate blood!' Ana talks with her hands. Then, seeming to remember that we're sitting in a Scandi-miminalist open-plan communal workspace in Denmark, she reins herself in slightly, adding in a lowered voice: 'We're not *great* at holding back in Costa Rica, we don't do "reserved" as a rule, so for Scandinavians…' Here she stops, before summarising tactfully: 'Let's just say life in Costa Rica is more noisy, more happy, more *relaxed* than elsewhere.'

There's a saying that Latin American people don't walk through life, they dance, and Costa Ricans are no exception. 'Which is great,' says Ana, 'but sometimes dancing's just not appropriate.' She goes on to tell me about how *pura vida* doesn't always serve Costa Ricans brilliantly in a work environment. 'There's not much structure,' she admits.: 'And '"Costa Rican time" is infamous…' Running two hours late is the norm, something that 'drives foreigners crazy', but Costa Ricans don't view tardiness as a mark of disrespect: they're just too chilled to clock-watch. 'There's almost a pride in this in Costa Rica,' says Ana. 'A lot of people see it as part of our charm – like "we have our own time"! *Pura vida* means that we can be a little too cool, sometimes.'

There are bigger problems, too. Twenty per cent of the population live in poverty and youth unemployment hovers around 25 per cent. San José, the capital, is one of the worst air-polluted cities of Latin America, despite the country's commitment to the environment. 'The roads are also terrible and driving in Costa Rica is an extreme sport,' says Ana, 'but we don't do anything about it – we're too relaxed. We just think, "That's the way it is".' Costa Rica is a predominantly Catholic country, ' – and I think this plays into why *pura vida* is so strong and why we're so relaxed about a lot of things,' says Ana. 'There's this idea that "if it will be, it will be". Or that "God has decided" and it won't make much difference what we do either way.' And yet on some issues Costa Ricans are prepared to take a stand.

Despite their relaxed temperament, Costa Ricans have a strong idea of the kind of people they want to be and are often described as 'the happy rebels of Latin America'. The Costa Rican military was disbanded by president and noted pacifist José Figueres in 1948 because he felt that government money would be better spent on education, health and eco-tourism. And he was right. Costa Rica has been a peaceful multiparty democracy since 1949, with high levels of literacy, near-universal access to healthcare, and a thriving ecology that attracts millions of visitors from all over the world. Abolishing the military had a significant impact on everyday Costa Ricans, too, changing the way they view the world and their approach to resolving conflict. 'We take pride in being citizens of a country that got rid of its army,' Ana tells me, 'and it makes us feel that we can achieve things via democracy and negotiation.'

Pura vida is about happiness and enjoying life, which usually means taking it easy and relaxing. But if your friends are in trouble, or if they aren't getting to live their *pura vida*, then Latin hackles are raised. 'If someone is threatening to take away the freedom and *pura vida* for our friends, we won't have it,' says Ana. Loyalty demands action and the normally carefree Costa Ricans tip out of their hammocks to take a stand. Like in April 2018, when voters turned out in larger-than-usual numbers to elect Carlos Alvarado Quesada in a landslide victory over the right-wing, socially conservative Fabricio Alvarado Muñoz, who was running to oppose same-sex marriage. 'We have this reputation for being laid-back – and it's true – but when we have a sense that something is wrong, we do something about it,' says Ana. Purpose and having a sense of meaning have both been shown to be important indicators for well-being and *pura vida*'s inner core of fierce loyalty helps keep Costa Ricans happy.

This combination of cool nonchalance, an emphasis on family (inherited or acquired), plus the ability to spend time in outstanding nature all year around, brings Costa Ricans pure joy – or *pura vida*. It's a lot like Aristotle's idea of *eudaimonia*, best described as 'fulfilment' or a state of contentment – basically, being happy and healthy. Contemporary scientists call this type of happiness 'experienced happiness or positive affect'. Or, as Ana puts it: 'People don't talk much about happiness in Costa Rica – we just live it.' At its heart, *pura vida* is a perfect alchemy of day-to-day 'carefreeness' combined with a social conscience and ecological pride. While we can't all relocate to the land of sunshine, tree frogs, turtles, and teachers who dote on us decades on (though I'm still hoping Ana's family might adopt me), we can all emulate the *pura vida* attributes, wherever we are.

HOW TO EXPERIENCE *PURA VIDA*

1

Try to relax more. Easier said than done, right? Spend time with the people you find most restful - the ones who are never in a rush. Make them sit down and tell you their secret...

2

Enjoy the outdoors and soak up your surroundings. No tree frogs? No problem: I bet there's a pretty interesting beetle or at the very least an ant nearby that can be marvelled at.

3

Consider adopting Costa Rican time, though preferably not on a work day, and see how different you feel without clock-watching constraints.

4

Look out for your friends and stand up for them. Stay cool until the time comes to turn up the heat. Because *pura vida* is for everyone.

rbejdsglæde (pro-nounced 'ah-bides-glull'), noun, a word that encapsulates the Danish attitude to work. From *arbejde*, the Danish for 'work', and *glæde*, the word for 'happiness', it literally means 'happiness at work' – something that's essential to living the good life for Scandinavians. The word exists exclusively in Nordic languages and the concept doesn't appear to be in force anywhere else in the world.

DENMARK

My neighbour – let's call him Lars to spare his blushes and mine – is a teacher in his mid-forties with a fine head of silver hair and the swagger of a man half his age. Lars works 'full time' ostensibly, but at some point between 9 a.m. and 3 p.m. each day, he will go for a long run, whatever the weather, then reward himself with a post-stretch cigarette on his front step as he watches the world go by. I know this, because I work from a desk in the front room of our house and 'watching the world/Lars go by' is what I do daily. Lars is a man who, in winter, can regularly be found in the street picking a snowball fight with whoever's passing. In summer, he'll retrieve a Frisbee from our garden most days (he has quite the forearm). Lars likes his job and is a man who appears to have his work–life balance well and truly sorted.

When we first moved in next door, I presumed that Lars was something of an anomaly. Then I met Mads and Mette, as they shall be known, who live in the house on the other side of us. Both have jobs they love but that can also be incredibly demanding. And yet... at 10.30 a.m. on a Tuesday both are home, near giddy with Zen, roll mats under their arms, having just come back from 'couples yoga'. Mads gives me a cheery wave over the garden fence and updates me on the progress of his downward dog, before telling he's just taken up a salsa class of an evening. They have three young children, a busy social life, and jobs that would be ball-breaking in any other country and yet the pair of them seem in a near permanent state of barbecuing and bush-maintenance. Introducing work–life balance, Danish-style, and the sacred art of *arbejdsglæde*.

'Most Danes expect to be happy at work,' my friend Karina tells me. 'You spend so much of your life working, you may as well enjoy it.' And *arbejdsglæde* is all about enjoying your 9–5 (or, rather, 8 a.m. until three-ish in Denmark). What helps is that Danes can study for free – and even get paid to do so over the age of eighteen – so more people can train to get jobs in fields they're interested in. And because of the sky-high taxes, the majority of Danes aren't primarily motivated by money so they opt for a job they actually like. Although the official working week is thirty-seven hours, recent OECD figures show that the average Dane is only working thirty-three hours a week. Denmark's 'Holiday Act' (everyone's favourite act) entitles employees to five weeks of paid holiday per year in addition to the endless days off for bank holidays, training, national celebrations and pretty much anything else Danes can think of. There are thirteen of these at the last count; with justifications as nebulous as 'General Prayer Day' (you know: for all your non-specific praying) – so Danes are guaranteed a day off to kick back every few weeks.

Once you finally make it to the office in Denmark, you seldom break a sweat. It's a pretty pleasant place to be, with very little hierarchy and everyone working together, as equals, towards a common goal. Much of Scandinavia is still governed by something called Jante Law – ten rules for living as outlined in Danish–Norwegian author Aksel Sandemose's 1933 novel *A Fugitive Crosses his Tracks*. The first of these translates roughly as 'you're not to think you are anything special' with the following nine essentially beating you over the head with the first in different iterations in the hope that by number #10 you will be under no misconceptions about the fact that individual success is an affront to Scandinavia's socialist principles and showing off is tantamount to murder. It's basically a 'don't be too

anything' manifesto, but the Danes – in common with the Swedes and the Norwegians – have bought it wholesale. Dress codes tend towards the informal and you won't see many ties in Denmark (I saw one for the first time in years last Monday. It was quite an event...). It's not unusual to see the CEO chatting to the cleaner around the coffee machine or the finance director waiting her turn behind the receptionist in the lunch queue. It's totally accepted that you can confront your boss or call out a colleague, and. as Karina tells me: 'If I have something to say, I can say it – to anyone I want to.'

This lack of hierarchy starts in schools, with children calling teachers by their first names and addressing them as equals, and even *whispers it* challenging them. 'It's absolutely expected that you'll tell a teacher your opinions on something,' says Karina in a tone that implies you'd be a dullard not to. 'From the start of life in Denmark, we say it like it is.' This is true. She does. They all do. There's also a great love of consensus in Denmark and everyone gets a say. This means that most workers feel empowered and invested in the outcome of any given decision. They're given a good deal of autonomy over their tasks, too, and as long as the work gets done, there's little concern about how, where or when they do it (thus morning yoga/afternoon Frisbee). 'I'm trusted to do a good job and left alone to get on

with it,' is how Karina puts it. 'I have complete control over my role and no one says "you have to be in at 8 a.m. sharp".' So Danes may work seven-until-three one week ('or even two-ish') then do a bit more in the evening, or skip work altogether one morning. 'I might just need a couple of hours out of the office,' says Karina, 'so I'd probably put it in the calendar to let someone know, but I wouldn't have to ask anyone's permission: I'd just go.' This sounds radical but it's not uncommon in Denmark.

'*Arbejdsglæde* means you have the freedom to make your job work around your private life, which takes a lot of stress away and definitely makes us happier,' she says. For anyone who's still in the office at noon, lunch is a non-negotiable, heavily subsidised, communal affair eaten in a work canteen. For afters it's highly likely that there'll be a cake knocking around. In Denmark, birthday girls or boys bring in their own to share and co-workers repay the favour by festooning their desk with Danish flags. Once you've got over the initial alarm that your desk has been colonised (it's always the Danish flag, regardless of your nationality), there's usually a group singsong followed by chitchat. And by then it's probably nearing home time. There's not the same culture of presenteeism in Danish workplaces as you find elsewhere, and working until 7 p.m. is more likely to earn you a lecture on efficiency or time management than a pat on the back. So, come 4 p.m. everyone turns off their computers and goes home.

'By having that flexibility I'm more motivated and focused while I'm at work,' says Karina, who's also experienced work culture in the UK and Australia. 'Working in Denmark, I get more done and probably put in twenty per cent extra.' So Danes aren't working harder; they're working smarter. There's still workplace stress – but this is generally because Danes have been so thoroughly conditioned to expect *arbejdsglæde*: they expect work to be flexible and rewarding and to feel good about it. So if they're not, it's a red flag and action must be taken. Immediately. There isn't the same culture of 'soldiering on' if you're struggling, for fear that being honest about mental health problems will impact negatively on your career. In Denmark you get help: you take six months off, after which you're welcomed back into the fold.

Denmark's world-famous welfare state offers a suitably comfy safety net should things go awry – so losing your job isn't the end of the world. 'It means that you don't have to worry about anything,' says Karina, '– you know you're not going to end up on the streets. You know your health is in safe hands. And you know your kids will get a good education, all the way up to university, funded by taxes.' Unemployment insurance ensures that many workers get 90 per cent of their original salary for two years – so most Danes know they'll be 'OK' if they're out of work for a while. This is part of Denmark's 'flexicurity' model that means it's relatively easy for companies to make workers redundant, but there are generous unemployment benefits and retraining programmes funded by the government (via the whopping taxes) to help Danes get another job.

As Jacob from Copenhagen tells me, it's seldom 'just a job' in Denmark: 'We expect to thrive at work.' Danes demand joy, satisfaction and motivation from their salaried employment – as well as a nurturing social environment (I know: greedy or what?!). 'Little things, like communal breakfast for all employees on a Friday; celebrating birthdays and marking anniversaries; chatting with colleagues in the canteen during lunch; or just meeting by the coffee machine in the morning – all make the day more enjoyable,' says Jacob. And if the fun stops? 'In theory you can resign without having to worry too much about when a job opportunity next presents itself,' says Jacob. 'This means that the majority of people will only stay in a job that brings them joy and fulfilment – otherwise, why not move on or even retrain?'

Denmark has had a focus on lifelong learning since the 1800s and spends more on vocational education programmes than any other country in the OECD. There's a sense that even if you get sacked, you'll be all right. And once you stop being scared of getting fired or ending up destitute, it's amazing how much bolder you can be. There was a mutiny at the Danish toymaker Lego's HQ when management changed coffee suppliers and workers at Carlsberg, Denmark's best brewery (probably) – went on strike when bosses  took away 'free beer during working hours' (the swines...). But in Denmark, expectations are high – and they are, largely, met. 'We know we have it pretty good,' says Karina, who admits that she is the envy of all her friends overseas for the thirteen-week vacation she has coming up. *Wait, what? Thirteen weeks?* 'Uh-huh...' Karina tells me how she and her partner saved some parental leave after their second son was born and are planning to go travelling. Her son is now four, but in Denmark parents can hold back a chunk of their fifty-two weeks of leave until a child is nine years old. *Don't your colleagues hate you?* I can't help asking. 'No! Everyone will muck in and cover my work while I'm away,' she tells me, '– just as I would for them. It's expected that I'll be considerate, doing what I can beforehand and going at a time that isn't too busy.' *Well, la de da for you...* I'm happy for her. Really. Can't you tell?

'The point is, in Denmark we have a choice,' she adds, 'and *arbejdsglæde* is a prerequisite for living Danishly.' Although the word is also found in Norway and Sweden, it's Denmark that consistently tops the polls for happiness at work. A 2016 Universum's Global Workforce Happiness Index found that Denmark was the number one country for contented workers, based on employee satisfaction, willingness to recommend a current employer and likelihood to switch jobs in the near future. A study from the University of Aalborg found that 70 per cent of Danes 'agreed or strongly agreed' with the statement that they'd keep working even if they didn't need the money. Denmark also comes top in terms of worker motivation, according to The World Competitiveness Yearbook. At first I presumed that this made Danes massive slackers, but then I found out that workers are 12 per cent more productive when they're in a positive state of mind, according to research from the University of Warwick. Because employee happiness is vital for worker motivation, for delivering great results and for retaining talent. *Arbejdsglæde* helps make Denmark the fourth most productive country in the world, according to Expert Market data. And with a short working week, you can have a life and get on in life.

The philosopher Bertrand Russell (no relation, sadly) believed that leisure was an essential component to living the good life and described it as the time when 'the soul is refreshed' and 'civilisation is created'. Old Bertie proposed that we should all work just enough hours a day to meet our needs. This way, everyone gets time for work, rest and play – something the Danes have licked. So, come 4 p.m., my adopted countryfolk will be paddle boarding, or singing in a choir, or mountain biking, or playing Frisbee. Aggressively and across a busy road. Jacob has so many hobbies – cycling, kayaking, photography, cooking and baking, at the last count – it's a wonder he has any time for work. This balance between engaging work and rewarding play, supported by an infrastructure and culture that makes both possible, is a major reason Denmark is always dancing around the top of the happiness polls. It's a different, decidedly *eudaimonic* approach to the good life – but it's one that works. So now I prioritise *arbejdsglæde*. I make sure I enjoy work, then log off, guilt free, and play in the sun whenever possible. I just have to watch out for that Frisbee...

HOW TO GET MORE *ARBEJDSGLÆDE* IN YOUR LIFE, WHEREVER YOU ARE

1

Talk to your boss. We may not be able to change the infrastructure of our workplace or our nation's work culture overnight, but we can try. 'Suggest to your manager that they'll get more out of you if they're flexible,' says Karina. Or show them this chapter.

2

If you're the boss, talk to your employees. Take action and bring more *glæde* into everyone's *arbejde*.

3

Reframe your 9–5. No matter what our situation, we're all working for a reason, usually to contribute to our well-being or that of others. It may not be fun every day, but there's still a useful purpose in it and so a value. Remind yourself of this with a tactically positioned Post-it.

4

Make the most of your workmates. Friends make the day go faster and can cheer you up during the dreary bits. Ones who bring their own cake = a bonus.

5

Really don't like your job? Retrain on the side and work towards a new one. It's never too late to keep learning.

JOLLY

Jolly, adjective, meaning upbeat or cheerful and relating to one's manner or mood. Also used as in 'hockey sticks' or as an intensifier, as in 'good show'. A Middle English word from the Old French *jolif* (an earlier form of *joli* or 'pretty'), it was used by Geoffrey Chaucer in *The Canterbury Tales*. Today the word is inextricably linked to Englishness.

ENGLAND

From fruitcake to dog walks, Blitz spirit and boiled eggs with soldiers, the English love anything that makes them feel 'jolly'. Although the word may have been co-opted by Santa and 'the holidays' in the US, it's a characteristically English term at heart. By putting 'jolly' in front of any word in the dictionary, you can make yourself sound a lot like a WAAF from the 1940s or someone in a P. G. Wodehouse novel. The word is frequently used to amplify a sentiment of appreciation, as in 'a jolly good fellow' or

'a jolly fun night', while 'jolly good show' is used to express admiration for something that has been said or done. The peculiarly idiosyncratic phrase 'jolly hockey sticks' refers to a particularly hearty, sporty public schoolgirl type, as coined by the actress Beryl Reid in a 1950s radio programme *Educating Archie* (fun pub quiz fact). As with most things in England, there are strong class connotations. Those who utter the word out loud in modern times can often claim membership to the upper echelons of society, but as a sensibility, it's universal.

'Jolly' denotes a very English kind of cheerfulness that's something akin to godliness for your average Englishman or woman. While the idea of a stiff upper lip may be a cliché from bygone days, there are still plenty of English folk who'd prefer to talk about the weather than their feelings. A SIRC survey on the emotional state of the nation found that fewer than 20 per cent of the population admitted to having expressed an emotion in the previous twenty-four hours. By contrast, a whopping 56 per cent had talked about the weather – in the preceding *six hours*. This is because the clement climate is safe territory in England. It's never too hot, it's seldom too cold, there are no natural phenomena to speak of, and we're blessed with four uninspiringly mild and damp seasons, which other than necessitating wellingtons all year around, cause little concern for the most part. Once, it was windy enough to knock over our wheelie-bin, but that was a blip.

But what the weather really does in England is provide a conversation opener for all kinds of 'jolly' interactions, whereby we'll continue to talk until we feel confident about getting onto more serious topics. Once we've reached this pinnacle of intimacy, we'll hastily beat a swift retreat back to the weather again. Or perhaps the garden. Or our pets. Many Englishmen and women find it easier to express emotions for animals than they do for their fellow human beings (my father-in-law likes to communicate the state of his mental health by referring to the dog's disposition, for example). OK, so we're not plumbing the depths of our souls in these cursory chit-chats, but at the very least we'll have made a connection and hit up some serotonin from the basic human interaction. In this way, 'jolly' weather talk come downpour or light drizzle functions as a survival mechanism of sorts – a distraction from one's own vortex of despair. Because 'despair' isn't very English.

Take my friend Caroline. Caroline has had a lot on her plate lately. She makes cakes for a living and is in great demand, so I mean this literally as well as figuratively. But a combination of illness, money worries, family matters and a son who likes to draw on the sofa (he's my godson, so I'm calling it 'art') means that she's busy and, often, knackered. 'But there's no point moaning about it, is there?' she tells me one Tuesday morning as the rain hammers down outside. She is sunshine personified, pure joy in all its forms, but still – happily – prone to a good swear and several glasses of wine when occasion requires. She is, in my mind, all that is great about

England and a prime exemplar of jolliness. 'I think I was just born this way,' she says, 'but it's also a particularly English characteristic.' Because from 'The Laughing Policeman' to Monty Python's *Life of Brian*, we try to look on the bright side of life on the sceptred isle. 'I find it very difficult to be down for long,' admits Caroline. 'Even this morning, I was having a bit of a dip – family trouble, money trouble – and then I saw a dog trying to push a trolley outside Lidl and suddenly I was beaming: 'Look at that sweet little dog!' Or I'll be out walking and see a rabbit, and the day seems brighter: 'A bunny!' It's slightly mad really... But I think there is a character trait in the English that's good at finding the joy in the little things,' she says: 'It helps keep your pecker up.'

Caroline and I originally bonded twenty years ago over a love of *Mary Poppins*. You heard: POPPINS. Or rather, Julie Andrews in all of her incarnations. For the uninitiated, Dame Julie Andrews is an English actress, singer, and star of such greats as *The Sound of Music*, *Thoroughly Modern Millie* and of course, *Mary Poppins*, where she plays a 'practically perfect' English nanny. But there was nothing perfect about the actress's own start in life. Born into abject poverty, the result of an affair, she lived first with one stepfather and then a second, who turned out to be a violent alcoholic, according to her memoirs. But Julie remained 'jolly' throughout. From an early age, she was the possessor of a 'practically

perfect' singing voice that was lauded by all, but in true self-deprecating style, she would only comment of her four-octave range that 'the dogs would come for miles around'. Throughout her career, she avoided songs that were sad, depressing, upsetting, or written in a minor key, because these definitely weren't 'jolly' – preferring instead to sing scores that were 'bright and sunny'. Because when you're Mary Poppins, 'jolly' matters. In 1997 she underwent throat surgery for suspected nodules, but the operation went wrong and damaged her voice permanently, reducing her soaring soprano to a fragile alto. Ever the trooper, she refused to let this get her down and was quoted at the time as saying  that, at the very least, she could now 'sing the hell out of "Old Man River",' with its legendarily challenging low notes. Demonstrating a 'jolly', can-do, Blitz spirit, she reinvented herself as an author, speaker and actor and is now enjoying a career revival at the age of eighty-three (and still looking fabulous, just FYI). Julie, in case you're reading, Caroline and I salute you – now and forever – as the high priestess of 'jolly'.

So fond are the English of taking the cheerful approach that anyone who doesn't follow suit can often be vilified – or at the very least not invited around for tea and scones. 'I struggle to be around people who are a bit Debbie Downer,' Caroline admits: 'because I'm just not. I can't sustain that, and so when other people can I think, "Oh come on! Why are you still grumbling? It's been hours!"' I tell her I have a tendency to feel the same. Just this morning a mum on the school run gave me the side eye and before I could rationalise that maybe she was just having a bad day, I found myself muttering, 'Who burst your lilo?'

This bias towards the jolly and against the miserable is borne out by every children's story ever written. From *Winnie the Pooh*'s Eeyore to *Matilda*'s Miss Trunchbull and Mr McGregor in the Beatrix Potter books, it's a truth universally acknowledged that 'the grumpy ones are always the baddies,' as my son puts it. Instead of wallowing, there's a sense that we should all just get on with it – either by going for a brisk walk to release

endorphins, or having a cup of tea and a biscuit. Or laughing at a dog outside Lidl. Whatever we do, we should do it with the aim of getting over our malaise and getting back to being 'jolly'. Sulking is 'jolly bad form' and simmering with resentment or bearing a grudge is similarly frowned upon. 'You can be cross, of course,' says Caroline, 'but you'd better deal with it pretty ruddy quickly: get back to being jolly and go on with your day!'

This is an impulse that many of us growing up in England imbibed from an early age from grandparents who lived through the Second World War. 'Stiff upper lip and wartime Blitz spirit were very real concepts to them and these were passed down the generations,' remembers Caroline. It's something that stuck in the minds of anyone born before the early 1980s, and many of us try to pass these learnings on to our own children. That's not to say that we all view WWII with wistful nostalgia. We don't. And the English grapple with a near-permanent cloak of colonial guilt, having committed more than our fair share of 'foul play' under the auspices of 'The British Empire'. The cheerful 'keep calm and carry on' mentality isn't a caveat for evading culpability or ignoring the consequences of our actions. Nor is 'jolliness' an excuse for burying heads in sand (which probably belonged to someone else originally anyway...). But regardless of your views on the nation's sketchy past or military interventions in general, 'Blitz Spirit' was a prime example of a very particular kind of camaraderie, stoicism and determination.

The death of Princess Diana in 1997 was said to have ushered in a new, more emotional Britain and it was the first time that the English as a whole went into mourning – letting the tears run free and crying in plain sight of other human beings who were not family members (unheard of previously). This spectacular period of public mourning and outpouring of national grief came in a flood, and once the cork was out of the bottle, it couldn't be put back in. Reality TV shows now regularly show contestants weeping or whooping for joy and we're getting better (slowly) at showing our emotions, good and bad.

So is the very English quality of stiff-upper-lip cheerfulness and being 'jolly' on its way out? 'I don't think so,' says Caroline, who points out that for every new season of *The Voice* in the TV schedules there's Penelope Keith judging 'Village of the Year' or someone over sixty beetling about on a barge. We're learning to balance 'jolly' with actual emotions. Which is, apparently, an altogether healthier way to be. Our best-loved comedians are all purveyors of this special kind of jollity – and we do 'funny' like none other. The English take pride in their sense of humour and a few of my favourite things are being able to flick on the TV or radio or download

a podcast and hear some of the funniest people I've ever encountered, talking as though just to me, in that uniquely English tone and timbre. We love them because they are like us – or rather, the wittiest versions of us – sharp, spry and satirical but soldiering on, no matter what. At our best, we are all Stephen Fry. On a good day, in full jolly flow, we are all Jennifer Saunders. Or Tommy Cooper. Or Lenny Henry. At our finest, we are all Mel and Sue (non British readers: look 'em up).

'Being English will always be about being jolly,' is Caroline's prophecy (and she makes exceedingly good cakes so who am I to argue/jeopardise my future supplies?). 'Jolly' is *The Borrowers* or *Just a Minute*. Or a couple from *Hollyoaks* winning an Oscar and the resulting BBC news coverage repeatedly referring to co-director Chris Overton with the quip: 'better known as "cage fighter Liam"'. 'We love an underdog and we like our heroes to be self-deprecating,' Caroline observes. This much is true and explains why we're not great on gushy American Oscar acceptance speeches (*retch*). Many of us are too squeamish to accept praise of any kind but the plus side of this is that the English tend to stay fairly grounded and maintain a sense of perspective, if not defiance, in the face of adversity.

When four bombs exploded in London in July 2007, overseas observers assumed that life in England's capital would never be the same again. But the city carried on as normal for the most part; Londoners rejected government attempts to increase security and clampdown on terror suspects; and our multiracial capital continued to thrive. People who had never experienced Blitz spirit first hand, suddenly behaved just as their grandparents had done, nearly seven decades ago. Friends who were caught up in the fallout, on the 'next tube' or bus, reported a strange sense of camaraderie on the streets of London that day. This isn't to undermine the tragedy: it's just that 'jolly' is our modus operandi in good times and bad. Message boards set up in the US to offer condolences to the families of victims were soon hijacked by Londoners begging for the syrupy outpourings to cease, followed by satirical take-downs on the heartfelt poems written by our American cousins. For Londoners, this was an entirely appropriate response: the terrorists would not be permitted to 'win' by halting business as usual.

During another terror attack on London Bridge in 2017, a man was photographed running from the scene at Borough Market still clutching his half-drunk pint of lager. Later revealed to be a Liverpudlian called Paul, he was hailed as a symbol of resilience, encapsulating the English sense of humour and defiance. Just this year, the journalist George Monbiot, on learning he had prostate cancer, wrote in his column in the *Guardian* newspaper that he was still 'jolly' and determined to stay that way regardless because 'my shitstorm score is a mere two out of ten'. There are always people worse off, he ruminated, before referencing the archetypal English proverb: 'Cheer up, it could be worse'.

Cheerfulness in the face of adversity and dogged adherence to remaining jolly at all costs is a coping strategy that has largely served us well. We've learned that happiness isn't a constant and the bad things in life can't be avoided. Life will 'get us', whichever way we turn. When we're beset by tough times or feeling down, our aim should be to get back to a manageable, reasonable state – a level playing field (probably with jumpers for goalposts...) where we can catch our breath and recalibrate. Because happiness can bloom from there. And it is a 'bloom'. 'Jolly' is about slapping on a smile and making the best of what you've got. It's the fleeting moments of joy, and laughter, and dogs pushing trollies outside Lidl, that all of us can notice and celebrate. Happiness is in the small things. So stay 'jolly'.

HOW TO UP YOUR JOLLY-O-METER

1

Feeling wobbly? Pop the kettle on and have a cup of tea and a biscuit.
Very few problems seem as horrific after two Hobnobs. Fact.

2

Still feeling wobbly? Have a brisk walk to get the endorphins going and
see if you can spot a dog. Or a bunny. Or, for extra 'jolly' points, both.

3

Making conversation about the weather is better than
making no conversation at all – studies show that it's human interactions
and regular contact (of any kind) that keeps us sane, so crib
up on your cumulonimbus.

4

Keep things light; laugh as often as you can, and embrace satire, always.

KALSARIKÄNNIT

Kalsarikännit (pronounced 'Kal-sa-ri-kan-eet'), noun, is defined as 'drinking at home in your underwear with no intention of going out'. From the Finnish *kalsari*, meaning 'underpants', and *känni*, meaning 'state of inebriation', *kalsarikännit* is literally 'pants drunk'. The term first appeared in the 1990s, gaining popularity online in the early 2000s before being inducted into the Institute for the Languages of Finland's online dictionary in 2014. Forget 'Netflix and chill': in Finland, it's Netflix and *kalsarikännit*.

FINLAND

During a recent cold spell, a meme went around social media highlighting the differences in climate and character between various northern European nations. The Swedes described the chilly weather as the 'Snow Cannon'. The Brits called it the 'Beast from the East'. And the Finns called it: 'Wednesday'. Finns know 'cold'. In the north they have reindeer, waist-high snow and sunrises so beautiful they should have their own Instagram (search #suomi and weep...). In the south, they're too near the sea to get snow (thanks for nothing, Maritime Effect...) but it's still 'so cold your face hurts', according to my friend Tiina who hails from there. 'And it's dark. Most of the time...' I tell her she's really selling the place. 'On the plus side, it does mean you can go out in sweat pants and no make-up because no one can see you. Your nearest neighbour might be 20 km away so you're not going to bump into anyone anyway,' she tells me. *Every cloud...* 'But we're good at insulation,' she says. 'We wear a lot outside and then we make sure our homes are really warm.' This is something I've experienced to a milder extent living in Denmark: yes, it snows (regularly), but Danes don't do 'draughts' and once you get inside, you can strip off as far as your own personal comfort and prudishness permits. And when Finns get home after a hard day at the Nokia-wielding, heavy-metal-thrashing coalface of just 'being Finnish', they like to kick back and let it all hang out (very nearly) – indulging in a little *kalsarikännit*.

'You can explain *kalsarikännit* to anyone in any country, anywhere, and they'll instantly understand what it means and why it's fun,' Marianne tells me with a hint of pride. Marianne is from Helsinki and she and I were at university together. Marianne is a lot of fun. 'Everyone knows what *kalsarikännit* means in Finland,' she says, 'and we all have an idea of it growing up. But it's when you get to your thirties that it really comes into its own. You know – when you don't want to go out all the time: you don't want to have to dress up, or put on make-up, or go outside, but you still want a few beers. So you stay home and drink in your underwear – something everyone's done at some point, right?' *Wrong!* I tell her I have genuinely never had the pleasure. I'm also miffed she neglected to mention this game-changer until now ('That's twenty years of pants-drinking you've deprived me of!'). Still, despite the apparently excellent double-glazing in Finnish houses, I can't help wondering how stripping down all the way to your smalls can be classed as 'cosy'. *Wouldn't pyjamas be preferable? Or a slanket, perhaps?* 'No' is the resounding response.

'Finns also drink quite a lot.' Tiina gives me a look as though to imply that this may or may not be relevant in terms of how much they feel the cold when clad only in their underwear. I give her a look to convey that 'it *definitely* is'. Finns are among the biggest drinkers in Europe according to 2015 WHO data. 'You have to buy alcohol from special shops in Finland,' Tiina tells me, '– the strong stuff at least. So once you're drinking, you really go for it.' And with their 'booze thermals' on, Finns are just fine in their next-to-nothings. As a result, *kalsarikännit* is so celebrated that in 2017 it got its own emoji. The Finnish Foreign Ministry created the icon as part of a series that also included naked people in saunas; the Nokia 3310; and

head-banging heavy metal fans. But it was the icon depicting a man and a woman in their underwear, beer in hand, which proved most popular. Presumably because Finns were in need of a shorthand to save frostbitten fingers countrywide the faff of typing out *'kalsarikännit'* in full.

Kalsarikännit is typically a solo pursuit or is performed with a significant other, but any Finns feeling more sociable can warm themselves inside and out in one of Finland's 2 million saunas (that's one sauna for every 2.75 members of the population in Finland). 'Sauna culture is huge and often you'll drink a beer while you're in there,' says Tiina. A lot of clubs and sports events include a sauna night where you drink beer naked before jumping into a lake or rolling in the snow. But Finns can handle it, because alongside *kalsarikännit* they have *sisu* or 'persistence and determination regardless of consequence,' Tiina tells me. It's thanks to *sisu* that in 1939–40, an army of 350,000 Finns fought off one-million-strong Soviet forces. Twice. *Sisu* is how Finns cope during the long, dark winter with lows of minus 35 degrees Celsius. *Sisu* is chopping logs in a blizzard. Or insisting on listening to heavy metal music out of a misplaced sense of national pride despite the absence of any discernible melody. These are all characteristics often associated with macho culture, but Finland boasts one of the best records for gender equality worldwide.

In the 1850s, Finnish activists for women's rights demanded education for girls long before other countries got their act together, and Finland was the first country to allow unrestricted rights for women to vote and be elected to parliament in 1906. In 2000 Finland welcomed in the world's first female president, Tarja Halonen, and, according to a 2017 OECD report, Finland is the only country where dads spend more time with kids than mothers. As Tiina puts it: 'There's not too much difference between men and women in Finland – we're all pretty tough. We've had to be.'

Aside from the brutal climate, Finns have borne war, famine, and being ruled by Sweden for the best part of 700 years, before being ceded to Russia in 1809. The Finnish people only regained independence in 1917 and, as such, Finland is a relative baby in the nation stakes. 'We're a new country,' says Marianne. 'So we're still working out who we are in some respects.' But, by most metrics, Finland is growing up nicely. It's been ranked the safest and best-governed country in the world; the second most socially progressive and the third wealthiest. What's more, Finnish citizens enjoy the highest levels of personal freedom and an education system regularly ranked among the world's best. This is largely thanks to the fact that academics led the country's nationalist movement, and since independence almost 30 per cent of Finland's heads of state and government have been university professors. Education has always been a priority and there was even a 19th-century decree that a couple couldn't marry in the Lutheran Church before both passed a reading test. Sex for spelling = quite the incentive.

In short, what with *kalsarikännit* and *sisu*, Finns have it pretty good. Everyone's equal, their education is second to none, and they're world leaders at enjoying the simple things in life. 'There are loads of things Finns should be happy about,' admits Marianne, but the famed Finnish equality comes with its own challenges – because when the equilibrium is upset, there is

outrage. 'If you win the lottery in Finland for example,' she tells me, 'more people will be jealous than are happy for you. There's meant to be a secret society of lottery winners who can all chat together because everyone else hates them!' The country's highest 10,000 or so earners have their pay published annually in what has now been dubbed 'national envy day' and there's even a saying that a Finnish person would rather pay €100 than watch their neighbour receive €50. 'We're nice like that!' laughs Marianne.

'We know that this is silly and Finns want to get better,' she says. 'We're becoming conscious of the fact that we're not as happy as other Scandinavian nations and so things like self-help books are becoming increasingly popular.' Many Finns are also learning to celebrate what they have. 'Like our nature,' says Marianne. 'It's all around you in Finland. Nuuksio National Park is right by Helsinki, or you can drive an hour from the city and really be in the wild.' She tells me about a mutual friend's recent visit where they went blueberry picking and then made elk stew. I tell her that it sounds like something out of a children's book. 'It was nice,' she admits. 'We have to remind ourselves how good we have it in Finland and how great it is to be outside in nature. But I think most Finns, if they're honest, enjoy time by themselves inside, too. It's really good to get home.' To whip off your sweatpants and crack open a beer? 'Of course! We're Finns: we'll always have *kalsarikännit*.'

I'll drink to that.

HOW TO *KALSARIKÄNNIT* LIKE A FINN

1

Turn up the thermostat. Unless you live in a spectacularly well-insulated house in Finland, in which case, well done you.

2

Stock up. You're not going outside again for quite some time so you're going to need supplies: snacks, drinks, a sustaining box set of some kind and/or a suitable conversational sparring partner.

3

Wear comfy underwear. This isn't the time for a lacy thong or anything underwired.

4

Draw the curtains or shut your blinds before you begin. Otherwise your solo activity might become something of a spectator sport...

GEMÜTLICHKEIT

Gemütlichkeit (pro-nounced 'ghem-ud-lich-kait'), noun, or *gemütlich*, adjective, meaning 'cosy', 'comfort-inducing' or relating to a sense of belonging and social acceptance. From *Gemüt* meaning 'soul, heart and mind'; *lich*, which correlates to the English 'ly'; and the suffix *keit*, meaning 'ness'. First documented in 1892, the word became associated with a distinctly German set of traits. The English writer G. K. Chesterton mentions *Gemüt* in 1906, describing a German beer garden as 'the very epitome of *Gemütlichkeit*'.

GERMANY

Nina has baked. This is not unusual. Nina likes to bake. And cook. And parent two small children. And work full time. Nina is unfazed by anything and neatly arranges baby cutlery, baby food, a bib, wet wipes, and an improving selection of toys on the table before taking a sip of her coffee. 'Ahh, so *Gemütlichkeit*,' she tells me as I'm still scrambling around with a face full of scarf, two mewling infants and trailing shoelaces – late, as usual, for our mothers' group meeting. Nina is German. I, demonstrably, am not. '*Gemütlichkeit* means doing something good for your soul,' she tells me as I realise my jumper's on inside out. 'So if you're stressed, or sleep-deprived...' – she looks at me – 'it's having a rest.' *Noted.* 'If you're hungry, it's getting something nice to eat,' she edges the baked goods towards me. Because *Gemütlichkeit*, I learn, is something that comes on top of your basic needs – it should be special.

'It's also not a constant,' Nina tells me, 'so you can find something *gemütlich* one day because you're in the mood to receive it, then another day you might hate it.' *Gemütlichkeit* is subjective, so it won't be the same for everyone. And it's private – intimate, even – 'far more so than the Danish *hygge*,' says Nina. 'Plus we don't go on about it all the time.' Here she permits herself an eye roll. 'When it comes to *hygge*, Danes are far more touchy-feely and expressive.' I've never heard Danes called that before, but compared to their border-neighbours, it's all relative. And for Germans, being 'touchy-feely' is a little too lax, something that's frowned upon. 'It's great to experience *Gemütlichkeit*, but not too much,' is how Nina puts it. Because then you might actually *become gemütlich.*

'Calling someone *gemütlich* would mean they were lethargic – not very fast or dynamic,' says my friend Frauke from Hamburg. 'So if a colleague wasn't pulling their weight or if they were dawdling, holding everyone up, that would be seen as a bad thing.' Idleness is an act of transgression in Germany, where the Protestant work ethic is alive and well and held up as a goal for all – especially in North and East Germany. To understand why, we need a quick dip into that most controversial of rabbit holes: religion.

Ready?

Let's go...

Sixteenth-century monk Martin Luther thought we were all becoming a bit cocky and attempting to buy our way into heaven rather than working for it. At the time, the Roman Catholic Church reigned supreme in the West and doled out 'indulgences' to sinners in search of redemption. An 'indulgence' wasn't a get-out-of-jail-free card – that was what confession was for (relax: I'm Catholic, I can say this) – but rather a document allowing believers to reduce their punishment in purgatory (a bit like a doctor's waiting room for the afterlife). Traditionally, indulgences were obtained by praying a lot or playing 'pilgrimage bingo' whereby the repentant

 ticked off as many holy spots as they could manage. But then some bright spark realised it would be much more efficient to just buy your indulgences instead. This practice was officially banned in Germany, but continued on the sly and in 1517, a Dominican friar named Johann Tetzel started a sizeable campaign to sell indulgences to renovate St Peter's Basilica in Rome. Luther was LIVID. He rejected the teachings of the Roman Catholic Church in his *Ninety-five Theses* – a collection of guess how many grievances? – and kicked off the Protestant Reformation. Instead of securing a place in heaven via confession and ceremonial sacrament, Luther proposed hard work, discipline and frugality as the tenets to live by. This notion spread throughout much of northern Europe and even America – but it's in Germany that the Lutheran ethos and Protestant work ethic are most apparent. Long story short: Germans don't hang about in a *hygge*-obsessed candlelit fug like their Danish neighbours. Instead, they like to get *Gemütlichkeit* and get on, without ever becoming *gemütlich*.

Another difference in the German approach to life and *Gemütlichkeit* is the absence of nostalgia. In Denmark it's practically the law to reflect on previous *hyggelig* times when you meet someone you've hung out with before. 'But we don't do so much looking back with rose-tinted glasses in Germany,' says Nina, originally from Hanover. This is understandable. Most Germans are acutely aware of their country's place in the history of the 20th century and there's even a term for the struggle to overcome the negatives of the past. *Vergangenheitsbewältigung* describes the processes of attempting to remedy as far as possible the wrongs committed and move on from the guilt of the Second World War. Post-war, Germany was on its knees and paying back reparations to the rest of the world, but once the dismantling of German heavy industry ended in 1950,

West Germany's economic recovery was fast and furious (East Germany's journey is a whole other book). Reconstruction, or *Wiederaufbau*, began – and today Germany is the industrial powerhouse of Europe, single-handedly saving the Eurozone from collapse in 2012. Always near the top in the productivity leagues, modern Germany is famed for its efficiency and democracy. This vast country, with a population of 82 million, also brought the world *Lederhosen*; Black Forest gateau and the incomparable experience of driving down the *Autobahn* listening to German favourite David Hasselhoff on local radio. I mention this for two reasons: firstly because I hope – as long as I live – to never knowingly pass up an opportunity to use the word *'lederhosen'*. And secondly, to emphasise that, notwithstanding their endearing quirks, the Germans approach happiness in staggeringly practical and pacey fashion. Getting a picture of the German sensibility? Good.

'People sometimes think Germans are overly serious,' says Nina, 'but it's not that – it's just we take pride in working hard. Only then can the "fun" start.' Germans like to do things properly and don't approve of *Spassgesellschaft* – a consonant spaghetti of a word that means living a hedonistic life or 'losing focus at work'. It's a slur often levelled at millennials and can be used as a kind of a warning, says Nina, '– a sort of "Don't party

too hard or enjoy yourself too much" like people did before the 2008 financial crash.' The idea that the entire economic downturn of a decade ago can be laid at the feet of Gen X seems a little harsh, but I get the picture.

Hard work is at the heart of what it means to live a good life in Germany and even during times of celebration the ability to knuckle down is central. German wedding celebrations often kick off with the custom of *Polterabend* – smashing porcelain and then making the happy couple sweep up the shards. This is intended to teach them that they'll have to work together through difficult conditions of married life (who says romance is dead?). Or *Baumstammsägen*, the tradition of sawing wood at a wedding ceremony to represent the first obstacle the newly-weds must overcome, in a lifetime of inevitable future obstacles. Because nothing says 'love' like a log.

'First work, then pleasure, is pretty much the mantra in Germany,' says Frauke. 'We don't combine the two, nor do we expect work to be pleasurable – or *gemütlich*.' She explains how Germans can be very negative about their work but still be happy overall. 'Because work is there to be done – and done well – then you can relax and have time for yourself.' Unlike *hygge*, which permeates every area of Danish living, Germans would never use *Gemütlichkeit* to describe anything to do with work – and no one expects Danish-style *arbejdsglæde* in Germany. There's a clear distinction between work and home, and Frauke tells me how a lot of German happiness concepts are to do with 'stopping work to have nice times'. Thus *Feierabend*, from *Feier*, meaning 'celebration' and *Abend* or 'evening', which means the festive mood at the end of a working day. 'There's also *Feierabendbier*,' says Frauke: 'the same word but you add "*bier*" on the end', used to denote an after-work celebratory beer ('we like a composite noun in Germany').

Post-work and post-beer, you can get back to your home – something that has a special meaning for many Germans. *Zu Hause* means 'being at one's home' but *Zuhause*, all one word, means 'the place where you feel you belong', and this is an important word connected with happiness. Germany only become a reunited nation post-war with the tearing down of the Berlin Wall in 1989, and many Germans had wildly different experiences of growing up based on whether they were in the East or West of the country. Several studies show that the historic East–West divide even has an impact on the way many Germans are raised today. So where you're from, matters.

'Your *Zuhause* is about feeling part of something,' explains Frauke, '– having a spiritual home or more of a philosophical way of looking at where you feel "right" and "good".' But this isn't a binary thing: 'There's often a feeling that you shouldn't expect to have all your *Zuhause* needs met in one place,' she says. Just as in relationships, we shouldn't expect to have all our needs met by one person (that way madness/romcoms lie...) – it makes sense to have an idea of belonging as a dual- or even multiple- based affair, with more of us moving around nowadays than ever before. 'It's natural to have a yearning for another place,' says Frauke.

Once you've found a place where you feel you belong, and you've finished all work for the day, then you can really get *gemütlich*. A lot of Germans live in apartments, especially in the cities, but in the German psyche there's a real love of nature and a yearning to be outside. Fortunately, many flats come with a balcony so

that Germans can create their very own *gemütlichen* beer garden. 'We even have something called a *Ferien auf Balkonien* or "balcony vacation" in Germany,' says Frauke. Whereas the 'staycation' is often linked to lacking the finances to fly anywhere fancy, *Ferien auf Balkonien* are ubiquitous in Germany. 'Everyone does it,' she says, 'regardless of age or wealth. It's celebrated. You might treat yourself to some new plants for your balcony, then you take a week off work and just enjoy spending time there.'

Ensconced on their balconies, revelling in some well-earned *Gemütlichkeit*, Germans can withdraw even further if needed to an inner world of imaginative escapes. 'You know when you sit on a table and swing your legs?' Frauke asks. I tell her that I do, but that I haven't done it for years... 'Exactly!' she says. 'It feels free and childlike. Right? Well the Germans have a phrase for also doing this with your soul: *Die Seele baumeln lassen.*' This jewel of an expression is apparently something you might say to a friend who's been stressed at work and has some time off coming up, for example: 'Have a really good break: let your soul swing!' Another favourite German phrase is *Löcher in die Luft starren* or 'looking at holes into the air', a little like staring into space; or *Kopfkino* – 'head cinema' – so daydreaming or having a fantasy. I tell Frauke I feel like I'm getting it: so work first then kick back and swing your legs/soul? 'Yes!' she tells me: 'Only not for too long.' *Sorry?* 'We also organise our leisure time. We might say "OK so we're going to let our soul swing, but we're going to do it for forty-five minutes…".' Ah, the joy of structured fun!

Frauke describes the German approach to punctuality and order as being, 'like a piece of string that pulls everyone along – we never let it all hang out.' There's even a term for it: *Freizeitstress* – or 'free time stress'. 'It's like: "Come on! We need to pack our bags for the beach!"' Frauke tells me, aware as she's saying it that it sounds slightly odd. 'But it's unavoidable – we have a work-like approach to organising our leisure and we just feel it pays to be prepared.' I am in no position to quarrel. I have been friends with Frauke for six years now and have never once been on an outing with her where all food, snacks, coffee flasks and wet-weather gear were not perfectly packed in preparation for every eventuality, leaving me feeling more shambling than usual. 'The cliché of Germans being honest, reliable and efficient is pretty accurate,' Nina agrees. 'In Germany we value education, facts and learning – and we like things to be done well.' Germans do the job, thoroughly, and then get on with the secondary occupation of having a good time (also a lot like a job in Germany. See: *Freizeitstress*).

Happiness in Germany is about the ordered cessation of work and taking a break to indulge – but it's also an individual thing. 'It's not about

family and friends or parental responsibilities,' adds Frauke. 'If anything, it's about breaks from them.' And this is OK: because you've earned it. Although parents have an expectation of duty towards their children, in German culture they don't typically assume that they will get anything back. 'I don't expect that my kids will take care of me when I'm older,' says Frauke, 'and on the whole, Germans don't expect anyone else to make them happy – we expect to work at it. We know it's up to us. It's a Protestant thing I guess – we have to do it ourselves.'

I don't compare one of my best friends to Nietzsche lightly, but here goes: the German philosopher (Nietzsche, not Frauke) argued that all of us are only ever in control of our own thoughts and actions. No one else's are our responsibility and there's nothing we can do about other people being regularly ridiculous (I'm paraphrasing...did you guess?). His rallying cry to accept life as it is and take full responsibility for our own actions, doing our best at all times, seems to encompass the German approach to life and happiness. 'It's simple really,' says Nina: 'you work hard, then you can play hard – and get *gemütlich*.'

HOW TO EXPERIENCE *GEMÜTLICHKEIT* AND GET HAPPY, GERMAN-STYLE

1

Pay attention to the things that soothe your *Gemüt* and make time
for more of them (Home-made biscuits? Baked.
Power nap? Off for one now).

2

...then channel Nietzsche and accept the things you can't change
(crabby colleagues, the weather, or your spouse's mood are none of
your concern). Work your socks off, then rest. Properly.
Take pride in the knowledge that you have done all you can.
There is satisfaction in a day well spent.

3

Got a balcony? Get *gemütlich* on it with a *Feierabendbier*. Ta da!
Your very own beer garden!

4

Let your soul swing (for a set period of time...). Everyone can spare
five minutes for a good hole-stare or head-cinema mini-feature.
See? You're more refreshed already.

MERAKI

Meraki (pronounced 'may-rah-kee'), a noun that can be used as an adverb (strap in...), the word entered Greek from the Turkish *merak* (or 'labour of love'). Its meaning evolved into the concept of precision, devotion and undivided attention applied to tasks – usually, creative or artistic. An introspective, precise expression of care and love.

GREECE

Greece: the country of Dionysus; dancing with a glass on your head; dancing on the beach à la *Zorba the Greek*; dancing while drinking ouzo (the anise-scented liquor I still can't smell without remembering a particularly potent night in 1997) and just dancing in general. Greeks know how to have a good time, but alongside the big, exuberant, party spirit, there's a quieter, more contemplative way of pursuing pleasure and happiness in Greece that's less well known beyond the country's 13,676 km coastline. *Meraki* is the idea of pouring yourself into something with love, care and passion – a precise, soul-enhancing pursuit that Greeks have excelled at for millennia.

Dimitra, a painter and historian from Athens who recently relocated to rural Denmark in winter (having had enough of all the 'sunshine' and Socrates...), says, '*Meraki* is about passion. It isn't about whipping something together – it's doing it with attention and love and perhaps, even, a note of perfectionism. It means –' here she presses her fingers together – '"precise". Or "deliberate". It's doing something with your soul.' As a painter, she tells me about a recent exhibition she gave at a local Greek-run venue. Dimitra worked on all the pieces with *meraki* and was just arranging them on the walls of the venue when the owner appeared. 'She looked around at the pieces, then pointed at one and said, "You know, if that painting doesn't sell, I think you should do more work on it."' From anyone else this might have been interpreted as rude, but from a fellow Greek, Dimitra understood that it reflected a shared understanding of *meraki* ('that, and the trademark Greek honesty'). The owner knew something made with *meraki* when she saw it and shared Dimitra's sense of perfectionism and care for the creations. 'But anything can be done with *meraki*,' Dimitra tells me, 'like preparing a meal or even setting the table.' *Meraki* isn't about dialling it in, or multitasking with a side plate in one hand and a smartphone in the other: it's about focus. A dedication to the task at hand without distractions. 'I cook with *meraki* whenever I can,' says Angeliki, an architect from Athens, '–and for me, it's about creating something that I know will be enjoyed as well as the pleasure in taking the time to make it special.'

Having a passion that you take pride in can be of extra benefit to those who can't say the same for their primary occupation and *Meraki* can make life worthwhile if your daily grind feels like something of a Sisyphean task. Anyone familiar with Greek mythology may remember the tale of Sisyphus – condemned to rolling a rollicking big boulder up a hill, only to watch it trundle back down again every day. If this sounds a little like your nine-to-five, take heart. Many tasks that need to be taken care of on a day-to-day basis aren't particularly challenging or inspiring – from filing, to raising purchase orders or even some of the more gruelling aspects of parenting. But you can break up the never-ending cycle of mundane work with your own personal challenges – things that you're passionate about that you can genuinely look forward to doing. Your *meraki*. Had Sisyphus been into macramé, just for instance, things mightn't have seemed so blue. His week-to-view calendar could have looked more like this:

Monday: Boulder roll, break for a half hitch.
Tuesday: Boulder roll, knock off for a square knot...
...and so on.

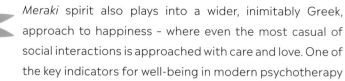 *Meraki* spirit also plays into a wider, inimitably Greek, approach to happiness – where even the most casual of social interactions is approached with care and love. One of the key indicators for well-being in modern psychotherapy is frequency of contact with friends and family, and Greeks habitually have this in abundance. 'It can take an hour to get home, even if you're already outside your front door, because friends or family will always stop and talk to you,' says Angeliki. Or, as Dimitra puts it, 'Greeks have been in each other's business forever.' Collective experiences are prized and Greeks don't do much alone. 'You'd never go to a coffee shop on your own, for example,' says Dimitra, 'and whenever something happens, I still call my friends straight away.' Here she mimes a phone in each hand. 'There's a sense of "Don't keep this in" and I think this is related to happiness – in the rest of the world, you might go to a psychologist to talk, but in Greece we talk to each other.'

Expressiveness is encouraged in Greece. 'Emotions are BIG and we even have unique words for expressions of emotions that you don't find elsewhere,' Dimitra tells me. My favourite of these is *klafsigelos* or the act of laughing yourself to tears. Greeks do 'sad' well, too. 'Greek tragedy isn't just a historical thing,' says Dimitra. ' If a loved one dies, you wear black; you mourn; you really wallow in it.' She tells me that in the village where her father comes from, you'd be shunned if you didn't wear black 'pretty much forever' following a bereavement. 'We weep; we wail; we dance; we sing – we do everything on a different scale,' says Dimitra. She's not kidding: the national anthem of Greece has 158 verses. That's *meraki*.

Theatre is also huge and there are 400 theatres in Athens alone. Even in remote villages of just 300 people, there's often a theatre. 'We go into depth about stories, which are all carefully crafted to reveal something about the human experience,' says Dimitra. Because: *meraki*. Tickets are affordable at around €10 a pop and performances are frequent, so it's accessible to all. 'Going to the theatre has always been a part of being Greek,' says Dimitra. She tells me that in ancient times, people would go to see a quadruple bill: 'You'd watch three tragedies for the catharsis, seeing things on stage that you'd never dare contemplate normally – like a mother killing her children in *Medea*, or a man sleeping with his mother in *Oedipus Rex*.' (You know, all the fun stuff us mothers get up to when we're not drinking wine at book club....) 'Then you'd finish up with a comedy.' Dimitra says: 'The idea was to purge anything negative or taboo, then get a lift at the end. Because the ancient Greeks really understood human psychology.'

Modern-day Greeks aren't doing too badly, either. Every child growing up in Greece gets to grips with their own mortality and sense of self from a spectacularly early age. 'You learn about Greek mythology from third grade in Greece [around age eight] and by the sixth grade [age eleven] you're on to Greek philosophers,' says Dimitra. 'You study the history of your country everywhere, right? It's just in Greece, our history is longer!' Children are regularly reminded that the goddess Athena 'helps those who help themselves' and most Greek teenagers are familiar with 'Plato's cave analogy' or even 'the story of Amphora' (no, me neither...must try harder).

'Greeks have a grounding in philosophy and – ultimately – psychology,' says Dimitra. 'So we have sunshine and the Mediterranean diet and extended family and all the things that have been proven to improve well-being and we also have a deep understanding of what happiness is and what it means.' And your *meraki* means that even on the days when life isn't going your way – when things feel hard or even boring – you've got something to look forward to. Your side hustle, your passion, can keep you going.

Greeks recognise that while we can't necessarily control what is happening around us economically and politically, we can control how we react to events and our own mood. To do something with *meraki* is to take time out from modern life to create and craft with attention and care. The people of Greece haven't had it easy historically, what with foreign occupation, wars and substantial economic difficulties that continue to this day – but still, for the most part, people are happy. 'We have a good quality of life,' says Angeliki, 'we don't stress as much as other people. There are some things we can't change, but we're pretty philosophical about that. We keep on going, finding ways to be happy – we make time for friends, and we make time for *meraki*.' You should, too.

HOW TO EXPERIENCE *MERAKI*

1

Turn your phone off and dedicate your time to focusing on one creative endeavour for the next ten minutes.

2

Cook something with care, if that's your thing; otherwise treat yourself to a takeaway but set the table to make it as elegant as possible. Napkin in the shape of a swan? Yes please...

3

Enjoy pushing yourself to finish a project in the best way you can. Perfectionism is only a negative if it's making you stressed – and *meraki* is about passion.

4

Haven't found your outlet yet? Try a few out. Hobbies make us happier – and being present as well as focusing on the task at hand ticks the mindfulness box as well. Win win.

ALOHA

loha, noun, meaning love, compassion, sympathy, kindness, respect and forgiveness – thought to date back AD 500, when Polynesian settlers first arrived on the islands. Hawaiian scholar Mary Kawena Pukui wrote that the first expression of *aloha* was the love between a parent and child. Commonly used as a greeting, but also a way of life in Hawaii – a guiding set of principles for interactions with the natural world and every creature in it.

HAWAII

The birthplace of Barack Obama and surfing, Hawaii is already punching above its weight in terms of cool. But *aloha* is 'without doubt' Hawaii's most important export, says Rob, a friend of a friend from Oahu who is to be my guide to a place that, in the words (almost) of James Taylor, I've never been to but would really rather like to go. OK, so Hawaii isn't a country in its own right, but it's snuck its way in on the basis of having its own island culture and being different from the rest of the US in more ways than there are pages in this book. And also because: *Hawaii*. Palm trees, pineapples, sea, sand, hula dancing and lei – or flower garlands – there's little not to love about the tiny US state in the middle of the Pacific Ocean, yet it's the Hawaiian spirit of *aloha* that makes its people so happy. And they are happy. According to Gallup studies, Hawaii residents ranked No. 1 for the highest well-being in the US and only 32.1 per cent of Hawaiians admit to feeling stressed on any given day.

'Aloha is so simple yet so complex in its meaning,' says Rob, '– because of the actions it obliges you to take.' He describes these in terms of a kind of selfless love and a sense of responsibility that I can't help thinking sounds a lot like the parent–child relationship Kawena Pukui wrote about. '"Aloha spirit" is often used to describe the warm welcoming vibe that folks in and from Hawaii have,' he adds. *And is it genuine?* I find myself asking, cynical Brit that I am. 'Oh yes!' Rob insists: 'It's completely pure and organic in origin, connected to the islands' nature, its people and the values of true Hawaiian culture.'

Zane, a pro surfer from Lahaina, agrees: 'Aloha is a way to go about living life. It's so much more than just a greeting: it's kindness and harmony and humility and patience and perseverance and being agreeable. Always.'

I'm fascinated by this. Simply 'being nice to each other' doesn't normally get much airtime in happiness research. There aren't many comparative well-being studies or investigations into the eudaimonic theory of goal hierarchy that kick off with a tick box marked, 'Bob was a bit off with me at lunch...' or 'Jill had a right face on her...'. But Zane's right: agreeability is an undervalued human trait. And although we all know by now that happiness is supposed to come from within (don't we?), it's always preferable to be around people who are 'agreeable' than a herd of old Eeyores. 'Because who are you to bring someone else down with your bad mood?' asks Zane. Fair point. He tells me that even when Hawaiians are having a bad day, they can call on their *aloha* spirit to 'up their game' and see them through.

The most common way to greet someone in Hawaii is with the *shaka* – a three-fingered wave whereby the middle two fingers are pressed down and the other three wave proud. The *shaka* is said to have started when a friendly old man, who always liked to wave at passers-by, lost his middle fingers in a gardening accident. 'This could have made him mad or depressed, but this guy had such a big heart, he always waved anyway with his injured hand,' says Zane. People waved back, and started to press down their middle fingers down too, in solidarity. The gesture caught on and a Hawaiian TV news reporter used this wave to sign off at the end of his show. 'His catchphrase was something like "Tune in next time for another shocker"', explains Zane, 'and with a Pidgin accent this came out as "shaka", so the name stuck.' Now the *shaka* is an everyday way to show *aloha* spirit to someone. 'They'll throw you a *shaka* across the beach and you'll throw one back, to acknowledge them and show your appreciation,' he says. And appreciation is everything in Hawaiian culture.

Early Hawaiians had an exceptional respect for the environment and an intuitive understanding of the eco-system – long before we knew the science behind it. 'The very first settlers would look out to sea and observe that the world didn't just start at the horizon – it started in the heavens,' says Zane. They could see water being drawn to the clouds when it evaporates, then watch it rain down to feed the rivers as the water takes its journey to the sea. 'Water is sacred in Hawaii,' Zane tells me. 'It's the lifeline of the land and water and the health of the forest and the coral reef. We have an ancient proverb, *ola alla wai*, or "water is life", and we live by it.'

For centuries Hawaiians lived in harmony with their surroundings, thanks to *aloha* spirit. 'There is an amazing balance between the land and its people,' agrees Rob. 'Hawaiians don't feel that they own the land – instead we belong to the islands,' is how he puts it. As such, Hawaiians feel responsible for every aspect of the islands' well-being. *Kuleana*, or 'taking care of the environment' is something that all Hawaiians grow up feeling is their duty, as well as making *pono* or 'respectful' choices that will benefit the community, the environment and the greater good. Hawaii's state motto is: *Ua Mau ke Ea o ka 'Āina i ka Pono*, which translates as 'the life of the land is perpetuated in righteousness' and this summarises the relationship between the people and the land. Hawaii's main island is divided into wedge shapes by the water running from the mountain tops to the reefs and Hawaiians would traditionally farm their 'slice' of the island in a cooperative set-up. The community shared resources and worked in synergy with the natural rhythms of land and sea. This system of working together meant plenty of leisure time for recreation – so much so that they even developed the act of wave riding into an art form. And everyone in Hawaii is a surfer.

'I have a life-long romance with the ocean and surfing was definitely my biggest passion growing up,' says Rob. Zane describes the ocean as his 'church' and is so accomplished on a board that he can even do handstands mid-wave (I don't know much about surfing, but I can't do handstands *on dry land*, so this seems impressive). Surfing as we know it today originated in Hawaii, and Duke Paoa Kahinu Mokoe Hulikohola Kahanamoku was the first to bring the sport to the rest of the world at the start of the 20th century. Researching into 'The Duke' further (not a chore), I find pictures of him playing golf while surfing (he's *that* good at surfing – as well as golf); surfing while a lady-friend stands Wonder Woman-style on his shoulders, and several where he looks as though he's trying to impregnate you through the camera lens (at least, this was my take home...). A regular Renaissance Man, The Duke also found time to be a law enforcement officer, an actor, a beach volleyball player, a businessman and a multiple-medal-winning Olympic swimmer – making the rest of us feel like quite the slackers. So how does this fit with the easy-going surfer mentality? 'Oh, you have to work, too,' says Zane. 'Working, fishing, playing – whatever you're up to, you're always doing it as well as you can and having a good time, too. Not necessarily joking about all the time, but doing it with a good attitude and with respect.' Because that's *aloha* spirit – something Hawaiians have clung to throughout their turbulent history.

After the Polynesian settlers arrived 1,500 years ago, having

navigated the ocean using only the stars, the Spanish rocked up in the 1600s, followed by Captain Cook in 1778, fresh from bothering the Australians. Contact with Europeans had disastrous consequences for the islanders thanks to an influx of new diseases and soon after this American Protestant missionaries arrived, determined to 'save some souls' and denouncing the traditional Polynesian hula dance as 'heathen'. The Kingdom of Hawaii was founded in 1795 with the unification of Hawai'i, O'ahu, Maui, Moloka'i, and Lāna'i islands, then in 1891, Hawaii welcomed its first and last queen, Liliuokalani. But less than two years into her reign, the US forced Liliuokalani to abdicate and relinquish all future claims to the throne. She was made to endure trial by military tribunal in her own throne room, before being sentenced to five years' hard labour. Liliuokalani was eventually pardoned in 1896 but in 1898 the Hawaiian Islands were officially annexed by the United States. At this point, the Hawaiian language was entirely banned from schools and government offices and by 1920 the Native Hawaiian population had dwindled to just under 24,000, according to the US Census. It wasn't until a constitutional amendment was passed in 1978 that it was once again legal to teach Hawaiian in schools and the Hawaiian Immersion Programme began in 1987. 'Today, Hawaiian is starting to be taught again to everyone, but for a lot of people the language of the country they call home completely passed them by,' says Zane.

From a population of 1.4 million, just 141,000 people identified themselves as being solely 'Native Hawaiian' in a recent census. Only a small proportion of Hawaiians today can trace their ancestry back to the original Polynesian settlers, but there is a commitment to preserving and promoting traditional culture. Haleaka Iolani Pule Dooley or 'Aunty Aka' was one of the world's best-known figures from traditional Hawaiian culture and a woman who helped share *aloha* spirit wherever she went. A 43rd-generation Hawaiian and the direct descendant of Hawaii's highest Ali'i (chiefs/chiefesses) and Kahuna Nui (the highest order of priest/priestesses), she was born into a home with twenty other children in Honolulu in 1965. Haleaka was raised without electricity, television, or any modern conveniences and instructed in the knowledge of her ancestors. She was trained to teach and share traditional Hawaiian wisdom with the world as a historian and healer and described *aloha* in one of her many YouTube tutorials as, 'a symbiotic relationship and an acknowledgement of that relationship you have with everything in the universe around you, and recognizing exactly what your space within that is'. Haleaka performed the post-inaugural native Hawaiian blessing of President Barack Obama and worked until her death in 2014 to promote *aloha* spirit, popularising Hawaiian proverbs such as:

> *He 'Olina Leo Ka Ke Aloha* – 'Joy is in the voice of love'
> *'A'ohe loa i ka hana a ke aloha* – 'Distance is ignored by love'
> ...and my favourite:
> *Ua ola no i ka pane a ke aloha* – 'There is life in a kindly reply'

Because being kind matters and compassion is king in *aloha* spirit. Acceptance is another central attribute and this makes for a philosophical approach to one's current circumstances, as well as those past. Haleaka once described a conversation she had with her grandmother about the 'discovery' of the Hawaiian Islands by Captain Cook. When she quizzed her elder on how to reconcile the concept of *aloha* with the great harm done to the Hawaiian people, she was told: 'How else will the world learn about *aloha*? How else will we remember that it is our innate sense to love things unconditionally?' This is a message Haleaka went on to adopt and propagate all over the world, telling audiences of Yoga Hub TV (a phenomenon of which I was hitherto ignorant) in 2014 that: 'Challenges are our greatest teachers – they show us what we really are.'

Today's Hawaiians still face plenty of challenges and some fear that the *aloha* spirit is under threat. Every year the islands attract in excess of 8 million tourists, who bring in money on the one hand, but great swathes of new development on the other. 'The genuine *aloha* that I grew up with is at risk of being drowned out by the noise associated with the influx of massive developments and people,' says Rob. He worries that this is putting a strain on what has historically been an easy-going and productive island nation. As a result, many in the sovereign movement in Hawaii harbour sour feelings towards tourism. 'We've had trouble with the water rights, too,' says Zane, 'with streams being diverted and islands losing their coral reefs – because just as bees pollinate plants, ocean currents pick up different pollens from these reefs and spread them.' But Zane remains optimistic. 'We're trying to reach out, to teach them,' he says, 'and we'll keep trying. Because *aloha* is about harmony, compassion and respect. So as long as this spirit continues, we'll do OK.'

And there's the rub. *Aloha* means going about your day making decisions that you know are going to benefit not only yourself but your family, your land, your friends and culture, and so the collective well-being of the community. This is happiness in Hawaii. Something that makes its culture beloved worldwide. 'There's so much warmth wherever you go when you're Hawaiian,' says Zane. 'When I say where I'm from, people light up – there's a lot of goodwill towards the place. It's like *aloha* spirit can be felt even by people who don't fully understand it. And that's pretty special.'

HOW TO KINDLE YOUR OWN
ALOHA SPIRIT

1

Acknowledge the people you meet and greet them with a
warm, welcoming, open heart.

2

Respect your surroundings. Yesterday I picked up litter on a beach walk
because I got sick of hearing myself *tut* about it and thought I should
take action instead. Today I spotted someone else clearing up, too.

3

Be more agreeable. Try bringing 'nice' back and see what happens.

4

Reconnect with the water. Take up surfing. Find a kayaking class.
Or just go for a swim and see how your body thanks you for it.

Þetta reddast (pronounced *'tah-tah-rah-dost'*) or 'it will all work out' is Iceland's motto. The phrase characterises a nation of modern-day Vikings who are easy-going with a core of grit – an unusual yet powerful combination. When faced with difficulties, Icelanders maintain a belief that things will be OK in the end; no matter how big the problem, a solution will always present itself. *Þetta reddast* means resilience. It means countering a financial crash by banging pots and pans. It means knowing that, in spite of the odds and, frankly, insane weather, Icelanders are capable of greatness.

ICELAND

Immersed in cloudy water, covered by silicon and minerals that have risen 2 km from below the earth, Reykjavik's Blue Lagoon feels like a giant bath of hot milk. Nearby, steaming, sulphurous water spurts from the ground, but drive south and you'll see mountains, black sand, waterfalls and glaciers. Iceland's extraordinary landscape is also extraordinarily forbidding, with lows of minus 25 degrees Celsius and only four hours of daylight in winter. Sunshine is such a rarity, even in summer, that workers get an ad hoc *sólarfrí* or 'sun holiday' to savour an uncharacteristically sunny day or 'an Icelandic heatwave' of 18 degrees Celsius plus. It's a climate so brutal, and a landscape so otherworldly, that in 1965 NASA dispatched Apollo astronauts to Iceland to train for their upcoming moonwalk.

'It's harsh,' admits Siggi, a digital consultant from Reykjavik, 'but then, we're tough – we've had to be.' Birna, an occupational psychologist, agrees: 'Icelanders made their home in an inhospitable land – but we made it our home. We made it work. We grew up telling ourselves: *Þetta reddast.*' Iceland is regularly voted one of the happiest countries in the world and Siggi and Birna are friends of mine and two of the most excellent human beings one could ever hope to meet. They're also married. To each other. Well done them. The Icelandic DNA that courses through them and their 330,000 fellow countrymen and women has served Iceland well and spawned such luminaries as Björk; Sigur Rós; Halldór Laxness; Arnaldur Indriðason; Yrsa Sigurðardóttir; the first democratically elected female president in Vigdís Finnbogadóttir; and the first openly gay head of government in Jóhanna Sigurðardóttir. And it's not just the people who are impressive. Icelandic horses – a strong, muscular, shaggy breed – are so Viking-esque that they stay outside all year around without blankets or shelter, eating only what they can find. Now that's tough. Basically, as a nation, Iceland has long been nailing it. And then came 2008 – a year that screwed many nations the world over, but none more so than Iceland.

The country's three major banks collapsed, resulting in the biggest banking crash experienced by any country, ever, relative to its size. An economic depression followed, along with political unrest and anger at government corruption and mishandling of the economy. But this was when Icelanders showed the rest of the world their *Þetta reddast*. 'The financial crash was an extremely tough time and we really counted on our resilience,' says Siggi. 'We don't go out and protest at just anything in Iceland – but in the crisis, we did. We were there every weekend, saying "We won't have this".' Icelanders never felt powerless. 'Instead, we took action,' Birna says, 'armed with pots and pans to bang, we marched down to Austurvöllur Square – the home of the Icelandic parliament – every Saturday to demand change.' The resulting 'Pots and Pans Revolution' called for the resignation of government officials and for new elections to be held. And they were. A new government was formed and by mid-2012, Iceland was one of Europe's recovery success stories. Not only did the nation's overall happiness dip only slightly during the crisis, but 25 per cent of Icelanders reported greater levels of happiness than before.

'This is because we proved to ourselves what we knew we were capable of,' says Birna. 'It was a case of *Þetta reddast.*' 'Resilience is rooted in our DNA,' agrees Siggi. 'The Vikings came to Iceland and had to live in the darkness and in really cold weather, so we had to survive.'

Now, Icelandic children are raised to be resilient. Children are made to walk long distances from an early age and taught to be outside, whatever the weather. Because if kids didn't go out in all weather in Iceland, they wouldn't go outside in winter at all. And trust levels are so high it's not unusual to see six-year-olds walking to school alone in the winter darkness.

The climate also brings with it a strong interior life. 'When it's dark all the time, you're driven to tell stories. Then in summer there is near-constant light, which makes people behave differently,' Birna tells me. 'It's hard to sleep, for one thing, but it also engages the imagination.' The ideas of *Þetta reddast* are woven into the stories Icelanders have been telling themselves for thousands of years and the country has a rich literary culture that dates back to the sagas, Viking tales of heroism in the face of adversity. There are also mystical stories of elves – or Huldufólk (hidden people) – that have been part of Icelandic history since the Vikings first landed on the island in 1000 AD. Today, 54 per cent of Icelanders believe in elves and 90 per cent are 'open to the idea' according to Magnus Skarphedinsson, headmaster of Reykjavik Elf School (who, I concede, may be biased). The stories that Icelanders tell their children also help to foster a *Þetta reddast* mentality. Instead of Santa Claus at Christmas, Icelandic kids have the Yule lads – thirteen half-trolls with names like

'Door-Slammer', 'Doorway-Sniffer', and 'Window-Peeper'who are supposed to visit children in the run-up to Christmas and play pranks. I tell Birna and Siggi that these sound a little creepy but Birna tells me that's nothing: 'There's also the

Christmas Cat, who eats kids that don't get new clothes.' *Woah there...* 'Yeah, it seems pretty harsh now but I think it was to encourage parents to knit a new sock...' Needless to say, Icelanders are also in touch with their dark side. No saccharine Disney-fied children's' stories here.

Another thing that helps Iceland rank highly on the happiness lists is the fact that they're big readers. Brain scans have shown that when we read, we mentally rehearse the activities, sights and sounds of a story, stimulating our neural pathways. Getting immersed in a book has also been proven to improve empathy and even levels of well-being. *Blindur er bóklaus maður* is a common term in Iceland and means: 'a man without a book is blind'. 'Because books have a special place in our hearts – you cannot overstate the importance of books in Iceland,' says Siggi. There's a tradition of exchanging books on Christmas Eve and an annual *jolabokaflod*, or 'Christmas book flood', when the majority of books are sold between September and December in preparation for Christmas giving. Every home gets a free catalogue of new publications called the *bokatidindi* and Siggi becomes misty-eyed recalling how he would pore over this as a child, circling the ones he wanted (much like British kids of the 1980s with an Argos catalogue). As a result of this passion for the written word, the country has more writers, more books published and more books read, per head, than anywhere else in the world. According to a BBC article, one in ten Icelanders will publish a book during their lifetime and there's a running joke that one day they'll erect a statue in Reykjavik to honour the only Icelander who never wrote a book.

This is another example of *Þetta reddast*. 'We don't see any obstacles to doing something if we want it,' explains Birna. So if you want to write a book or run a marathon, you just do it. *Þetta reddast*: it'll all work out. 'I think this self-belief is something to do with being the original Vikings,' says Birna. 'We're the rebels, fleeing mainland Europe and making a place that didn't seem an obviously hospitable habitat our home. Because of this, we think we're special. I believe I am capable of greatness because I am Icelandic. We know we can make things happen and we're taught to think like this growing up – we have a certain spark that carries us forward.' I've never wanted to be Icelandic so much in my life. 'And this self-belief pays off,' she adds. 'Look at our football team, how did that happen?' she laughs. I know nothing about football but even I am vaguely aware that the Icelandic team do 'all right'. 'Or crossfit,' Siggi goes on, '– three of the four fittest women on earth are from Iceland. It's insane!'

He's not wrong. Worth an inspirational Instagram follow are Katrín Tanja Davíðsdóttir, Annie Thorisdóttir, and Elmóður – meaning 'fire heart'. And that's what all Icelanders seem to have – a fire in their heart that no sub-zero temperatures or snowstorm can extinguish. 'We are tough,' says Birna, 'we're resilient and we have an attitude to life of *Þetta reddast* – so we can do anything!'

HOW TO DEVELOP A
ÞETTA REDDAST MINDSET

1

Think positive. If Icelanders can stay upbeat while essentially living in a fridge for most of the year, so can you.

2

Be creative – work with what you've got and make a virtue out of those long winter nights.

3

If the outside world is inhospitable, cultivate your inner life.
Read a book – or make like an Icelander and write one.

4

Get strong, Viking style. Work out, flex your muscles, and, crucially, take fish oil. Icelanders swear by it for mood-boosting properties and general health. Capsules are acceptable but for purists, stick to the spoon. 'There's a saying in Icelandic: "You're not a man amongst men if you don't take it from the bottle",' Siggi tells me ('But take it first thing, before you eat anything, to avoid fish burps,' Birna cautions).
The glossy-haired Viking-spirited revolution starts here...

JUGAAD

Jugaad (pronounced 'juu-gard'), noun or verb, a colloquial Hindi term used to mean frugal innovation, a 'hack', or an attitude and commitment to getting things done – no matter how. Named after the trucks cobbled together from parts of old army jeeps discarded in the 1950s, *jugaad* has come to represent improvisational ingenuity and resourcefulness. A distinctively Indian philosophy to make the best of what you've got.

INDIA

My friend Fatema grew up in a modest house just outside Mumbai with her two younger siblings, her parents, her grandparents, her aunt and uncle, and two cousins. 'There were eleven of us under one roof and so although living this way brought us a lot of joy, in such close quarters we also had to do some *jugaad.*' Tolerance and forgiveness were lessons learned early on but it was near impossible to carve out any personal space and Fatema never had a room to herself. 'I would crash on a mattress in the living room at night, which was fine, but I always wanted a wall,' she says. *A wall?* 'Where I could put up my posters and stickers and things. It was the 1980s, you know...' I nod: I know. Stickers were my everything circa 1988. 'I couldn't put things up in the living room as we had to keep that spick and span for visitors,' Fatema tells me, 'so my mum did some *jugaad* – she allocated me a cabinet that had to look neat on the outside but when you opened the doors, inside was my space,' she beams at the recollection. Fatema's husband is also a *jugaad* aficionado. He grew up in the Goan countryside where there were no toyshops, '– so he used to make his own out of things he found in the forest'. *He made his own toys?* I look around at my son's embarrassment of Lego riches. 'Of course: that's *jugaad.*'

This isn't uncommon. Another acquaintance, Sid from Chennai, used to make cricket bats out coconut tree branches. 'We also made toast and a fried egg on a clothes iron,' he tells me. This worked but was, unsurprisingly, messy. 'Second time round, we improved it with a metal dinner plate on top of the iron. Worked like a charm.'

Jugaad – or the Indian spirit of improvisation, ingenuity and resourcefulness – means finding a quick fix and doing whatever is in your capacity to reach your goal. 'It might not be perfect but you'll get there,' says Fatema. It is, to summon the bloated ghosts of 1970s management consultants, the ultimate in 'thinking outside the box'. And it's a way of life in India. Fatema got on a plane to leave India for the first time in 2014. She now lives up the road from me and we go to a 'free-dance' class together, an activity that she nails (because: *jugaad*) while I scuttle up and down like a terrified crab (because: English). But her new vantage point on her home country from a distance of 6,616 km away has unleashed some fascinating insights. She tells me now how interesting it was to observe the way the Western world looks to the East for spirituality and the idea that there's more to life than material things. 'This is despite the fact that everyone in the West still wants more material things and many Indians haven't got enough materially to survive.' But she also noticed that the *jugaad* approach to life that she'd previously taken for granted was an asset. '*Jugaad* is about making things happen instead of just sitting and waiting for the ideal situation or conditions – and Indians are good at everyday ingenuity and taking a practical approach.' In other words: getting shit done.

'So I might say at work, "I'll do some *jugaad*",' says Fatema, 'and it just means, "I'll figure something out".' *Jugaad* decrees that you'll do your best to ensure a positive outcome. 'But if something doesn't go our way or turn out as we hoped, we don't sulk: we try something else. We don't have time to sit and brood: brooding is a luxury. So you go to plan B.' With a population of 1.3 billion, there is competition for resources in India and so every opportunity is maximised, via *jugaad*. Fatema tells me about the auto-rickshaws she used to take to get to prayer school in her hometown, where drivers would improvise an extra seat in the hope of another fare. 'They'd create a sort of DIY ledge next to the driver, or they'd attach a tiny

wooden plank in front of the normal passenger seat, cram three little kids on it and call it a "school bus".' Outside observers were often alarmed by this. 'But in India it is forgiven,' she says, 'because you get a ride and the driver gets to earn a little more.'

You don't always need more resources: you can innovate within constraints and create something to fulfil your needs for the moment. 'I don't tend to panic under pressure in my personal life or at work, for example,' says Fatema, 'because I always find a way.' There is a confidence that this is a viable course of action, and *jugaad* is a refreshing contrast to the archetypally female affliction of impostor syndrome. I can't help thinking that every workplace needs a Fatema, and indeed, *jugaad* is an approach that has been extolled by management gurus in recent years. Researchers at the University of Cambridge claimed that *jugaad* could not only benefit emerging economies, it could serve as a way out of the financial crisis for developed economies who needed to become better at flexible, creative thinking and using fewer resources. Which is all very well, but there's a danger, too, in romanticising the roots of the concept. As Fatema says, 'many Indians are living by *jugaad* because they have no choice.'

According to the late US psychologist Abraham Maslow, there is a five-tier hierarchy of human needs, each of which needs to be met before you can move on to worrying about other things. These needs start with the basics (food, water, sleep etc.), followed by 'safety' (security of body, health and employment). Both of these need to be in place before you can move onto 'belonging' (friendship and intimacy), then the fourth, 'self-esteem', and finally to something called self-actualisation – the highest thing we are all aiming for in life: an understanding of 'Who am I? What am

I for?' But in India, the triangle is inverted. 'Spirituality is very important and self-actualisation is something people are familiar with in India, but many are struggling to meet their basic needs,' says Fatema. The best things in life may well be free, but studies from Princeton University and Purdue University show that money *can* buy us happiness up to a certain level. This satiation point varies between countries and studies (around $75,000–$95,000 in the US), but the figure should guarantee enough financial security to take care of our basic needs and leave us feeling comfortably well-off. Even taking into account geographical variants, the average income in India falls far short of 'comfortable'. If you get sick in India, the quality of the hospital you go to and the care you get depends on how much money you have. In this respect, money is directly proportional to happiness. And here lies the catch.

'Indians aren't doing *jugaad* because it makes them more creative – they're doing it because of lack of opportunity,' says Parmesh Shahani, fellow author and head of the Godrej India Culture Lab in Mumbai: 'We make do with less, we manage, but it's not celebrated as a badge of resourcefulness in India – people have a *jugaad* mind-set to survive.' Resilience and fortitude are prerequisites to function. While researching his 2008 book, *Gay Bombay: Globalization, Love and (Be)longing in Contemporary India*, Parmesh discovered how *jugaad* is even more of a necessity in the LGBT community: 'We have creatively reimagined what it means to be in a gay relationship,' where people in long-term couplings are living in the closet with family and only seeing each other at weekends. 'This is because (a) it's still illegal and (b) there's still a lack of social acceptance in some places,' he tells me. Parmesh described this approach as

'relationship-*jugaad*' to reflect the fortitude and resilience of the LGBT community in India. 'But that was ten years ago – and nothing's changed,' he says. 'I don't want to have to "creatively reimagine" my relationship.' It's a stressful way to live but many can't bear the alternative – either not seeing their family or the person they love.

Poverty is widespread and there are 270 million Indians who don't have enough to meet their basic needs according to World Bank Data. 'Every new government comes with a promise but there's no investment,' says Parmesh, 'so *jugaad* isn't a choice for many in India.' Practising *jugaad* from a stable position is desirable. Practising it from need is not. 'But if you have food on the table and no one is going to throw you out for loving who you love, then *jugaad* is a good thing,' says Parmesh. Because in places where your basic needs are being met, *jugaad* can help you fly.

Fatema agrees: 'If you have the basics, *jugaad* can help you get to the top of Maslow's triangle. But you need the basics.' There is a cruel irony that the very Indian concept of *jugaad* as a philosophy for a happy, successful life works most effectively outside of India. We can all feel guilty about that. But we can also keep trying. To make the world a better place, be resilient and keep on keeping on, *jugaad* style. Things won't ever be perfect but just as the concept of the 'good enough' mother has saved the sanity of half of the human race, there's something to be

said for the 'good enough' attitude to life – creatively making the best of what we have. So do your best; be creative; transcend the norm; and don't just think 'outside' the box – burn it. Who needs boxes, anyway?

HOW TO *JUGAAD* IT

1

Innovate, within constraints. Haven't got a room of your own or even
a wall? Find a 'cabinet' equivalent that works for you, for now.

2

Do more with less. If life gives you a coconut branch,
whittle your own cricket bat.

3

Be flexible and think creatively. Want a fried egg sandwich? Fashion
your own metaphorical hotplate and make it happen.

4

Things not going to plan A? Try plan B. Never brood. Never sulk.
One of the greatest lessons for a happy life that any of us can
ever hope to master.

5

Imagine what would happen if you just said 'yes' more. Don't know how
to do a thing? I'll bet you know someone who can. Disregard impostor
syndrome, dismiss the fear, and do the thing anyway.

CRAIC

Craic, noun, derived from the Middle English term crak and used in 18th-century Scotland (by Robert Burns, no less) to mean 'conversation' or 'news'. The word reached England by the 19th century and became linked with gossip, before arriving in Northern Ireland mid-20th century. It was subsumed into the Irish language with a new Gaelic spelling – *'craic'* – but wasn't in widespread use until the 1970s when chat-show host Seán Bán Breathnach incorporated it into his catchphrase, *'Beidh ceol, caint agus craic againn!'* –'We'll have music, chat and *craic*!' Ever since, the term has been taken to include all of the above as well as 'generalised fun'. Usages include: 'What's the *craic*?' 'It was good *craic*' and 'The *craic* was mighty'.

IRELAND

A four-year-old terrier called Dinny ('short for 'Dennis'...') is sitting on a bar stool in County Wicklow looking a bit pleased with himself – as well he might. He is being serenaded, en masse, on a Monday night. My friend Niamh only popped out for a drink to give Dinny a walk, but now she's standing in a circle with twenty-five locals singing 'One Day More' from *Les Mis*. And there isn't a dry eye in the house. This is *craic*. An artist and interior stylist, originally from Dublin, Niamh is an astute observer of the world around her and, as such, she is the perfect guide to a word I can't even bring myself to say in my Home Counties accent ('It just doesn't sound right!' I tell Niamh. 'You're right: it really doesn't,' she agrees). So I let her say it. '"*Craic*" may be a relatively new term in Ireland, but we've always had *craic*, even before we got a name for it,' she says. Before the 1970s it was just thought of as 'being Irish', which isn't as catchy. So *craic* it became. And since Ireland always tops the UK in happiness surveys, it's fair to assume that there's something we can learn from the Emerald Isle.

'At its heart, *craic* is about storytelling,' Niamh tells me, '– whether through conversation or song or poetry, *craic* is about sharing experiences.' And it's everywhere. There are nights in the backs of pubs where people who want to tell a story get fifteen minutes, like an open mic spot without the mic, and there are ad hoc gatherings around the fireside in people's homes. 'The stories can be new – so gossip or the news of the day – or they

can be stories that go way back,' she says. 'There are stories I know inside out but never read myself, like "The Children of Lir", where a stepmother turns her children into swans, or the one I'm named after – "Niamh and the Land of the Ever Young".' Here, the eponymous heroine falls in love with a warrior from the mainland and brings him back to Ireland. 'But then he goes and gets homesick,' Niamh tells me, as though this is the kind of thing warriors are always going and doing. 'So she lends him a magic horse to go home on but tells him not to touch the ground. He's doing fine, but then he sees a man trying to move a rock so stops to help and – unsurprisingly – falls off.' The unlucky equestrian ages 300 years and never sees his love again. Bleak, certainly, but compelling enough to entrance generations, and these storytelling skills may even contribute to Ireland's enviable position in the happiness leagues. Psychologists from Oxford University have found that hearing harrowing tales of woe can help with group bonding as well as triggering endorphins as our body gets ready to fight off imagined 'pain' in real life. So getting scared or sharing sad stories in a group setting can, counter-intuitively, make us happier.

'Stories like this have been told by the fireside forever,' says Niamh. And this legacy has produced some of the greatest storytellers of all time. 'If you think about the number of writers and singers that have come out of a country of just 4.7 million people,' says Niamh, 'James Joyce, George Bernard Shaw – even Shane MacGowan [a second cousin

of Niamh's] is a wonderful poet. That creativity is in the blood and something that's encouraged growing up in Ireland. When I was a kid, you'd have your bag of crisps and a bottle of Coke with a paper straw and you'd listen while the grandparents told stories or sang songs in the pub.' Ah yes: the pub.

Ireland has become synonymous with pubs the world over and social drinkers will be delighted to learn that a trip to your local can also contribute to well-being. Researchers from the London School of Economics found that happiness levels increased by almost 11 per cent when a test group of selfless volunteers drank alcohol in a social environment. Ever the early adopters, the Irish have been getting in on the idea of a drink with friends as part of the *craic* for more than a thousand years and the oldest pub in Ireland is thought to date back to the 10th century in Athlone, County Westmeath. Even during the temperance movement in the 19th century, illegal drinking houses served *poitín* – a distilled potato liquor that averages between 40 and 90 per cent ABV (and comes in at number four in *Time* magazine's 'Top 10 Ridiculously Strong Drinks', just FYI). 'But the Irish hate being associated with drink and Guinness,' Niamh tells me, 'and besides, I'd say there's a lot more drinking in England.' She and I enjoyed the tail end of daytime drinking when we worked together in Richmond in the early 2000s, so I break it to her gently that times have changed: 'The two-hour Oyster-Bay-Chardonnay-and-a-chicken-baguette lunch is a thing of the past.' We both mourn its passing for a moment. 'Still,' she insists, '*craic*'s about stories more than getting sloshed.' Understood.

That's not to say that the Irish don't milk the hard-drinking, *Riverdance*-tapping, Daniel O'Donnell-crooning clichéd view of *craic* held by the rest of the world when it suits them. 'In Galway or County Kerry, some places really giddy it up for the touros... [tourists],' says Niamh, 'but generally in most small towns, the storytelling and the singing are enjoyed for real.' Modern technology has intruded a little on the atmosphere of times gone by and a lot of pubs now have a television ('or two') on in the background. 'They're usually showing sports or *The Weakest Link*, and it drives me nuts,' Niamh confides. 'But if you're having a really special time – singing or telling stories – they might mute it for you. That's the highest mark of respect in Ireland.'

This happened to Niamh the week before we speak. 'Some folk guys were playing music in a pub where there were only about four people,' she says. 'My other half volunteered me, saying, "Oh, Niamh can sing you something," and I thought, "Oh sure, I'll give them a song." If you have a voice it's your duty to use it – that's how we were brought up, you sing if someone asks you to. And then some others joined in and we wound up singing Irish ballads with endless verses. And I mean endless – if you didn't know the song at the start you did after verse seventeen.' Niamh and her newfound friends ended up singing until 3 a.m. These songs were only deemed over when someone yelled: 'Ahh, done!' and everyone tumbled home. This was prime *craic*, she tells me, 'spontaneous, special and inclusive – everyone is welcome and it doesn't have to be *Irish* stories or *Irish* songs (see *'Les Mis'*). At its best, *craic* is just...lovely. You can be totally moved and feel privileged to be a part of it.' Which sounds like a pretty appealing recipe for happiness.

'We're good at that in Ireland,' says Niamh, 'finding ways to be happy.' In the course of her work, Niamh restores a lot of old furniture and if she scratches the surface of most chairs or dressers from the past century, she finds a myriad of colour underneath. 'You can see that beneath the beige or grey or white, it's been bright yellow or grass green or electric blue. That says a lot about the Irish mentality for me – we've had tough times and terrible oppression, but we've found a way to stay positive.' This suffering has also engendered a sense of gratitude for all that is good and a readiness to celebrate even the everyday things. Like the uniquely Irish tradition of celebrating 'Women's Christmas' on 6 January. This date marks the end of the festive period in most Christian cultures, but in Ireland it's a special day where women get to let their hair down after toiling tirelessly over the holiday period. 'Obviously it's not great that women had been working their arses off for twelve days,' says Niamh: 'but it was about them deciding, "You know what? I've peeled enough potatoes now. I'm having the night off."' Essentially 6 January = International Women's Craic Day. You're welcome, world.

'We can be melancholy in Ireland but I'd say we're still happy,' says Niamh. 'I mean, we had 400 years of shite, between the famine and Cromwell, so we excel at being downtrodden. But we're also an independent nation. We had a hard recession but we've come out of it the other side and we know how to enjoy ourselves. We've had a lot to deal with but we're still smiling. And that's the *craic*.'

HOW TO EXPERIENCE *CRAIC*

1

Tell your story and listen when others tell you theirs.
Sitting next to a stranger at a wedding or at dinner? Delve deep.
Find out what makes them tick.

2

Watch a psychological thriller, see a scary play, or share tales of woe
with friends to build bonds, trigger endorphins and get happier.

3

Be spontaneous: see where the evening takes you. Those special,
unforgettable nights are seldom planned and never come with a curfew.

4

Sing your heart out. Until 3 a.m. if you can. Try worrying less about
your early start the next day and more about living your life, now.
Prioritise spending time with people over leading a controlled,
organised, colour-coded diarised life [memo to self...].

Dolce far niente – or the sweetness of doing nothing – from the Latin *dulcis* meaning 'sweet'; *facere*, meaning 'to make or do'; and *nec entem* – literally 'not a being'. Although difficult to determine when the phrase was first used (proponents were far too peaced-out to bother transcribing), the term appears in print in the memoirs of Casanova, the famous 18th-century Italian adventurer. Presumably when he eventually tired of all his carnal and geographical adventuring and needed a rest. Today, the term exists as a treasured concept that's seldom spoken out loud but oft hashtagged on Instagram accompanying pictures of Italians in hammocks. Casanova would be #proud.

ITALY

Forget Anita Ekberg paddling in the Trevi fountain at dawn in *La Dolce Vita*: think Fellini passed out in a hammock after the wrap party (probably). Or the vague sense memory of sitting in the shade on a summer's day long ago, before you became preoccupied with work, family and the hamster wheel of 'life'. *Dolce far niente* is a soul-expanding celebration of doing nothing – something that's actively discouraged in much of the world where the cult of 'busy' is ubiquitous. OK, so Italy hasn't exactly topped any happiness rankings in recent years, but the cliché of the carefree Italian still exists – and with good reason. Italians do 'nothing' like no other nation and perfecting the art takes style and skill – because there's more to it than meets the eye.

'*Dolce far niente* is almost an act of defiance for Italians,' says Francesco De Carlo, a comedian born and bred in Rome. 'We live in a country with a lot of corruption where we don't trust the law, or rules, or society... We don't even like the referee in football. And we LOVE football,' he tells me, 'so why shouldn't we opt out? Why shouldn't we take a break whenever we can to stay happy? We're also a relatively young nation, and I think this is significant,' Francesco adds: '– until 1861 we were ruled by other countries, so we're a little like a rebellious teenager!'

The Italians have a long and illustrious history of viewing authority figures with suspicion and demonstrating their disdain via satire – from the endless mockery of Berlusconi to Commedia dell'arte and the work of Dario Fo. Italy has faced more than its fair share of problems in recent years with the economy only just starting to emerge from its longest recession since the Second

World War. The financial crisis hit Italians hard and a 2013 study found that the poverty rate in Italy had almost doubled in the preceding five years. Unemployment is high and even for those in work, the job situation is precarious. Most Italians report having little faith in their politicians and a recent Istat survey concurred with Francesco, finding that almost 80 per cent of Italians didn't trust their fellow countrymen and women.

'Rome has always been a town of politics and parliament and the pope and corruption,' says Francesco. 'We don't feel like the state or society cares about us, so why should we care about them?' He tells me that *chissenefrega* is a word heard a lot in Italy – a term that roughly translates as 'who cares?' 'Of course we have emotions,' he clarifies. 'God, do we have emotions! We have love and passion and the mafia – it's as though extremes are the norm here. Have you driven in Italy? Even the cars fight each other on the roads.' I tell him I still have flashbacks to a four-vehicle altercation in Sicily circa 2013. 'So you know! There is chaos all around in Italy so the only thing you can depend on is friends and family,' says Francesco, adding that, 'happiness is in the little things'.

It's watching the world go by over coffee and a *cornetto*. It's laughing at tourists. Or politicians. Or the Pope. 'Or anything really,' says Francesco.

'We have to laugh or we'll cry so humour is very important. In Rome, especially, everyone is a comedian. The waiter bringing your coffee will stop and tell the whole restaurant a joke first. You just have to wait.' While the seconds tick by, instead of drumming fingers on a table or checking a phone incessantly, Italians will relax into the moment. That's *dolce far niente*. 'In the UK you're obsessed with schedules, with everything running on time,' Francesco shakes his head: 'People work a lot then they stop working and go crazy, drinking until they forget themselves.' I shift uncomfortably in my seat. 'But in Italy, we drink to enjoy ourselves. There's not so big a difference between working and not working for Italians and we don't worry too much about the future – *chissenefrega* – we just enjoy the present.'

This mode of thinking is revolutionary in its simplicity. Many of us search for relaxation by travelling to exotic locations, drinking to oblivion, or blotting out the noise of modern life with whatever our favoured crutch might be. But what if we were to let the chaos envelop us or sank into it like a hot bath? What if, instead of saving up our 'fun quota' for an annual escape, we spread it over the minutes, hours and days throughout the year and gave 'enjoying life' a go? The Italians seem to. Other significant words include *penichella*, similar to the Spanish *siesta*; *meriggiare*, a poetic term that means 'to pass the hottest hours of the day in the shade'; and *abbiocco*, a noun used to describe the sleepy feeling you get after a big meal. Drowsiness is such an art form in Italy that the phenomenon of doing nothing has been enshrined in the lexicon.

'It doesn't matter where you are from, we're good at *dolce far niente* everywhere in Italy,' says Chiara, a friend from Lake Maggiore

('not the one George Clooney hangs out at, the other one'). Chiara now lives in Denmark and works with other internationals who struggle with the concept of idleness. 'An Italian might say: "You're not doing anything tomorrow? Good for you!"' says Chiara, 'but Germans and Danes are horrified! They'll ask: "Why? Are you OK?" I try to explain that there's a pleasure in completely enjoying and savouring time – and for Italians, *dolce far niente* is a part of everyday life. But they never "get it"!' Italians won't say *"dolce far niente"* out loud, Chiara tells me, 'because the *"far"* part is an infinitive version of the word and so cannot be declared.' Obviously... 'It's more of a feeling,' she says, '– that and an Instagram hashtag.' There are currently 200,000 Instagram posts hashtagged *dolce far niente*. Hammocks feature heavily in half of them. Wine plays a significant role in the rest.

'In Italy, it would be perfectly normal for whoever you're with to declare at 5 p.m., "Hey! Let's all go get a glass of wine!",' Chiara tells me. 'You may have kids at home but we don't worry about that, because for one hour you'll enjoy time with the people you're with, whoever they are.' It doesn't matter if these people aren't particularly close – 'I might go for a beer with a person I go to the gym with, for example.' I tell her I love the idea of a beer as a 'gym chaser'.

Dolce far niente means 'enjoying the moment'. 'For me,' Chiara says, 'it's being in the shade with a glass of sparkling wine before lunch, maybe in August, when everyone is off work in Italy, and there's nothing to do but sit and eat.' There's often a drink involved and for many people, food plays a big part. I think about this, then ask: *But if you're eating, then surely someone's cooking?*

'Well...yes...' she tells me: 'that'll be your grandmother. Or rather, *someone's* grandmother.' Grandmothers may traditionally rule the family in Italy but they also feed the family. Chiara tells me that her husband's grandmother – 'Nonna' – is ninety-three years old and still insists on feeding everyone. 'Lasagne, *pasta al forno* – anything baked,' she tells me with a faraway look in her eye as she remembers pastas past. I tell her that this sounds like a lot of hard work and she tells me, 'That's nothing: Tuscan grandmothers wake at 5 a.m. to prepare the pasta, rolled in just the right way with the precise pressure in their fingertips.' And this is just an established side effect of *dolce far niente*? That someone else will be doing all the work? 'Pretty much' is the response. 'My mum is a grandmother now,' says Chiara, 'and she still has the rolling pin from her own grandmother. She tells me, 'This is the tool! One day, this will be yours!' Our grandmother lived with us and cooked for us growing up, and some of my best memories are with her, waiting for dinner as a child when she'd take the crust of the Parmesan that she wasn't using for cooking and dip it into the flame on the gas stove until it became chewy then wrap it in paper for us to eat...' she tails off and we both take a small interlude to compose ourselves, mouths watering. 'So yes, someone's always doing something, but it's not

us!' And when your time comes around to be a grandmother? 'Then it's accepted that you get to be the boss but you also have to do some cooking and childcare,' says Chiara. 'It's just how it is – but I wouldn't change anything!'

As a nation Italians are proud of their heritage – from the Roman Empire to the philosophers. Children are schooled in both of these growing up, but in adulthood there's just one ancient edict that Italians swear by: *carpe diem*. 'You still hear this Latin phrase a lot in Italy and there's a sense that tomorrow might never come, so you should live now – and, more importantly, spend now,' says Chiara. 'Status symbols are still very important to many Italians and there's an idea that "happiness" is a bigger car or a designer handbag. There is no concept of scaling back your life to within your means.' Immediate pleasure is often prioritised over long-term well-being and, as Chiara says, 'your status is more important than your bank balance – because appearances matter.'

This is something I remember well from my former life in glossy magazines, traipsing around New York, London, Milan and Paris for their respective fashion weeks. Milan was always the highlight for me, not just for the pasta and not because the clothes were the most stylish (they weren't: the French win this accolade). What I loved was the glorious riot of excess – the colours and opulence and sheer exuberance of a Versace show; the pure drama of Dolce & Gabbana (their flagship store/mansion is a sight to behold); and the over-the-top 'throw everything at a mannequin and see what sticks' approach of Valentino or Moschino. 'Minimalism doesn't exist in Italy,' says Chiara. 'I can spot an Italian in any country, anywhere in the world, in about five seconds.' Francesco agrees: 'We're peacocks.'

Italy is a country of contradictions. It's passion and idleness. It's having fun now and paying later. It's *carpe diem*, followed by Catholic guilt and some quality time in the confessional booth. 'There's a sense that our work will come,' says Chiara – just like her mother's rolling pin – and someone's always cooking. 'It's just that when you're experiencing *dolce far niente* it's not *you* having to do it. Not yet.' There's probably a bit more snoozing to do first. And perhaps a glass of Prosecco.

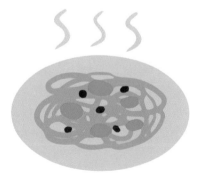

HOW TO EXPERIENCE
DOLCE FAR NIENTE

1

Take a day off, midweek, to do nothing. Don't tell anyone, lest they fill up the hours with plans (or worse: chores) and enjoy some *dolce far niente*.

2

Back in your 'normal' life? Instead of using your free moments to check your email or scrolling through Facebook to see what Sally from sales did on her holidays, try doing *nothing*.

3

I mean it: nothing. Log off in the evenings and at weekends.

4

Take a nap. When I go on holiday now, the thing I look forward to most is family naps. Really: bliss.

5

Still twitchy? Past midday and no serious health conditions to take into account? It's bound to be cocktail hour somewhere. Why not have a drink? Or some pasta? Or both? *Chissenefrega!*

WABI-SABI

Wabi-sabi (pronounced *'wah-be-sah-be'*), phrase from *wabi* meaning 'simplicity' and *sabi* meaning 'the beauty of age and wear', a worldview centred on the acceptance of transience and imperfection. The abandonment of all aesthetic ideals that demand 'perfection', *wabi-sabi* is an appreciation of things the way they are; a revelling in the texture and complexity of real life and the beauty of imperfection. Think asymmetrical faces, knobbly vegetables and cracked pots.

JAPAN

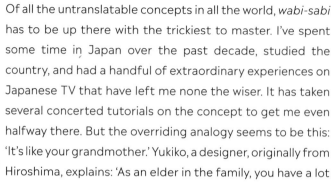

Of all the untranslatable concepts in all the world, *wabi-sabi* has to be up there with the trickiest to master. I've spent some time in Japan over the past decade, studied the country, and had a handful of extraordinary experiences on Japanese TV that have left me none the wiser. It has taken several concerted tutorials on the concept to get me even halfway there. But the overriding analogy seems to be this: 'It's like your grandmother.' Yukiko, a designer, originally from Hiroshima, explains: 'As an elder in the family, you have a lot of respect and being "old" isn't a bad thing in Japanese culture. It means you have a history, which adds value.' And with age comes wisdom. Which matters now, more than ever. Because despite having one of the longest life expectancies going, a staggeringly high GDP, and stacks of self-help tomes weighing down shelves in bookshops nationwide, Japan isn't a terribly happy country. Urban isolation and a widening gap between the ageing population and the young mean that many admit to feeling lost, stressed and anxious, much of the time. But by maintaining links to the past, not focusing on the shiny and new, and cherishing things that are old, a *wabi-sabi* approach to life might just be the answer.

Yukiko learned a lot from her grandmother growing up. 'She used to farm rice and she would say, "God exists in every grain of rice".' Yukiko was taught from an early age that respect for nature and the circle of life were key for contentedness, as well as being the basic principles of *wabi-sabi*. Yukiko used to help her grandmother in the rice fields and every day there'd be grass coming up around the sides of the field, taking nutrition and water from the rice. 'Every day, we cut it down,' she tells me, 'and then the next day, it would be back again. But that's nature! We learned to respect the power of the natural world and all its imperfections. It's always changing, and everything has a life cycle.' Sometimes crops come out well; sometimes they don't. Sometimes the weather will be conducive to a good harvest; sometimes it won't. But in Japanese culture you're grateful regardless – and you do the best with what you have.

'We learn to celebrate imperfections,' says Yukiko, 'and I think of *wabi-sabi* as being like the English word "patina".' Only in English, things aren't often valued for their patina. An old leather chair cracking on the arms? Upgrade. Laughter lines? Fill 'em. My stomach after three children? Wear muumuus forevermore (*'It's not that my skin is too big for me: it's "patina"'*, said no one ever). I raise this with Yukiko, who says, 'In Japan, it's different. We respect things becoming older and well used – from people to pottery.'

Kintsugi is the ancient Japanese art of repairing broken ceramics with metallic lacquer so that the cracks, far from being covered up or concealed, are highlighted in pure gold – celebrated, even. In *kintsugi*, the scar is gilded and the beauty is because of the imperfections, not in spite of them. The break is the beauty. *Kintsugi* treasures the old, reusing and elevating it to something with a higher value than the box-fresh new version. This is *wabi-sabi*.

But Japanese culture isn't always so forgiving of mistakes. 'We do not, as a rule, like failure,' Yukiko tells me. 'In Japan, we are so afraid to make mistakes that if tourists ask for directions, people who aren't so confident with their English will just say "No, sorry!" rather than risk making a mistake.' Mistakes at work are considered even more of a catastrophe. 'If it's something I can fix myself,

then maybe that's OK. Maybe... But if I have to speak to other people about it – friends, family, etc. – I am so ashamed,' she says. And herein lies the paradox. Japan is a homogenous society where high standards are the norm. These standards can appear 'perfectionist' to the rest of the world, but in Japan, they're commonplace. The Buddhist concepts of acceptance and 'letting go' are well known to all Japanese people in theory. But in practice, many Japanese people are taking diligence, attention to detail and conscientiousness to perilously competitive levels.

Karōshi, or 'death by overwork', is an occupational hazard in Japan, usually down to strokes, heart attacks or suicide. In its first white paper on *karōshi* in 2016, the government reported that one in five employees were at risk of death from overwork. The Japanese work significantly longer hours than the populations of other developed countries, and employees regularly take less than half of their annual holiday allowance – so workplace stress is rife. 'It's a big problem,' Yukiko concedes. 'Even some of our popular culture terms for things like "purpose in life" (*ikigai*) that seem, to the rest of the world, to be to do with happiness, are still about duty rather than enjoyment. So your *ikigai* might be your job or your family, but that doesn't mean these will make you happy – just that

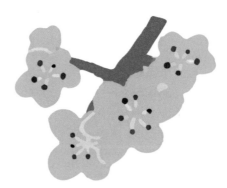

you'll work hard at them. And whatever Japanese people do, we tend to work hard at it.'

So where's the *wabi-sabi*? 'It's in the snatches of happiness,' Yukiko tells me. 'We work hard and then we retreat to nature to revitalise and charge up again. A lot of twenty- and thirty-somethings in the city tend to make an effort to get out into nature at weekends to get refreshed.'

Wabi-sabi decrees that there is a beauty and a profundity in bearing witness to the seasons – from fallen leaves to blossom scattered in the wind and rocks covered with moss. 'This calms the mind, relieves stress, and leaves us ready to return to our normal lives,' Yukiko tells me. Miyuki, a colleague from Tokyo, agrees, adding: 'the very imperfections of *wabi-sabi* seem closer to our human nature and so bestow a calmness, relaxing mind and spirit. When we feel *wabi-sabi* a stillness seems to visit our heart, even if only for a moment.' *Wabi-sabi* can also refresh the mind, 'giving us a different perspective on daily life', she says. So your meeting might have been a total disaster but the moss is starting to grow on your favourite tree in the forest or the buds on the pot plant on your windowsill are beginning to unfurl.

There's also a big emphasis on visiting *onsen* (hot springs) as well as *ohanami*, the cultural activity of gathering to appreciate flowers, specifically cherry blossoms. And then there's the wonderful Japanese custom of *shinrin-yoku* or 'forest bathing'. No water is required for 'forest bathing' – instead, it's like sunbathing, only in a forest, where the point is simply to be present in a woodland environment and really take it all in. A 2010 study from Japan's Chiba University found that participants who walked in a forest had lower blood pressure and lower levels of cortisol (the stress hormone) afterwards. Forest bathing has even been shown to change the cerebral activity in our brains in a way that promotes relaxation, according to a study from the Japan Society of Physiological Anthropology.

Dismiss all ideas of performative, picture-perfect, 'Getting out to nature #blessed'-type outward expressions of 'happiness' that we're bombarded with on Instagram – this is about recharging, restoring and spending time in the wild. After which you can go back to your busy job, your stressful commute, or your family, reinvigorated and ready to tackle whatever your day has in store. Instead of burning out, this is a sustainable way of living whereby you own your past and your present – reconciling yourself to both. Forget 'brand new you': this is about the old you, refreshed. *Wabi-sabi*, in fact.

'We don't always remember to do this on a daily basis,' says Yukiko, 'but this is the ideal – we cling to a *wabi-sabi* approach to be happy and stay sane. We know that this is the way to be healthy and to recharge'. So even if modern life becomes too busy and we're fearful of failure, *wabi-sabi* is a tool to 'reset' ourselves. I am not a weather-beaten wreck – a mere husk of my former self, held together by dry shampoo, coffee and willpower: I am a *kintsugi* creation of the highest order. We are all *wabi-sabi* masterpieces of our own making: our cracks and scars warrant gilding, for all to see.

HOW TO EXPERIENCE *WABI-SABI*

1

Appreciate the old, the lived-in and the pre-loved. From pensioners to pottery (and post-baby pouches...).

2

Create new value from something old and keep using it. Fix that broken bowl with *kintsugi*. Repurpose a piece of furniture. Make friends with sustainability, *wabi-sabi* style.

3

Find your recharging spot. In the forest, in a park, by a river, or anywhere that you can experience nature's asymmetry and wonder.

4

Tune in to the beauty of the natural world, both blossoming and on the wane – even if it's just by having a new houseplant on your windowsill. Notice the changing colour of the leaves and how the petals drop, one by one.

TŪRANGAWAEWAE & HAKA

Tūrangawaewae (pronounced *'tu-rung-a-why-why'*), noun, a Māori concept, from *tūranga* meaning 'standing place' and *waewae* meaning 'feet': literally 'a place to stand' or where one has the right to be. A word that has been around forever but that was first recorded in the 1960s. *Tūrangawaewae* has come to mean the places where we feel empowered and connected: where we experience a sense of identity, independence and belonging.

Haka, noun, a Māori ceremonial group song with accompanying synchronised movements, typically involving stamping, shouting and powerful gestures. Around since the 13th century when Polynesian settlers first arrived on the islands, *haka* was brought to a worldwide audience by New Zealand's sporting teams, notably the All Blacks who have been performing *haka* ahead of international rugby games since 1905.

NEW
ZEALAND

I'm squatting, barefoot in a room full of strangers, moving as one, chanting *'Ka mate, ka mate! ka ora! ka ora!'* and letting out thirty-eight years' worth of pent-up emotion. I feel rooted. Empowered. And oddly connected to the people around me, even though we only met this morning. I'm also convinced that I'm engaging in some grade-A cultural appropriation by performing *haka* as a Brit. But this, Kane Harnett-Mutu, from the Ngāti Kahu tribe of Northland tells me, is OK: 'Māori people have been educating Europeans for centuries...' He says this with a twinkle in his eye but there's truth in his words. Māori are often referred to as 'the only indigenous people the British couldn't overcome' and, unlike many cultures, they've survived largely intact. Unsurprisingly, it hasn't been easy. Which is why *tūrangawaewae* and *haka* are so crucial to Māori concepts of happiness and a life well lived.

In traditional Māori culture, nobody owns land. 'You have your *tūrangawaewae* – a place to stand – but everyone shares and you all work together to take care of the land for the next generation,' says Kane, explaining that a Māori's only role is to 'pass it on in a better condition than we receive it'. Which is lovely. But then the British came along (it's at this point that I habitually apologise on behalf of my ancestors). The arrival of Europeans to New Zealand in the 17th century brought enormous change but initial relations were amicable. The Brits endowed inalienable rights to the Māori people in 1840 in return for allowing European settlers to acquire resources and the two cultures coexisted. 'We adapted pretty well to the new arrivals – we're quick learners,' says Kane, ' and we incorporated the best bits of their culture, too.'

Then the Europeans got greedy (I know: so unlike us! Oh wait...). Rising tensions over disputed land led to conflict in the 1860s and the colonial government confiscated great tracts of Māori tribal land – leaving many without access to their *tūrangawaewae*. Things went from bad to worse (see Simon Schama or someone for a longer explanation) and a hundred years of oppression began. By the 1960s Māori elders were asking schools to restrict the use of the traditional language as they were concerned that it would hamper the next generation from entering the workplace. 'Inadvertently, we became a culture on the brink of dissemination,' says Kane, 'because without language, you can't sustain a culture.'

Tribal leaders throughout New Zealand began to realise that they needed to take action. 'We knew we couldn't depend on the government and so we'd have to depend on each other, to pool our resources,' says Kane. And so in 1982, the Te Kohanga Reo or 'language nest' project began, with Māori-speaking kindergartens set up where elders could look after younger children and teach them the language. By having a direct influence on the children, they could pass the culture down to the next generation. 'It bunny-hopped me and most forty- and fifty-somethings,' says Kane, now fifty-two, 'but anyone younger than me got the chance to learn Māori through newly developed community language courses or at school.' They also set up *kapa haka* (meaning '*haka* team') in schools, tertiary institutions and workplaces to teach *haka*.

'This wasn't because we were so angry or we suddenly wanted to go fight them,' Kane clarifies. 'People get the wrong idea about *haka*,' he explains. 'They see the All Blacks – a strong, confident unit of men going out and playing the game like a symphony – and they connect the power of *haka* with the aggressive nature of rugby. But take it away from the sports arena and you see what *haka* really means to Māori people.' There are hundreds of different types of *haka* in a variety of genres, with some written specifically for weddings, some performed predominantly by women, some written for children – there are even *hakas* to motivate employees in the workplace. '*Haka* isn't about aggression,' Kane assures me, 'and it isn't a macho thing.' He explains that strength and showing emotions are one and the same in Māori culture and that the posturing or *pūkana* – wild staring with eyes dilated, tongues often protruding - is used to emphasise particular words. 'It's about communication, unity and, ultimately, love,' he says.

Haka is performed to welcome distinguished guests, acknowledge great achievements, to mark joyous occasions or times of great sadness. But the outcome of *haka* is always unity and a re-connection of the body, mind and spirit. *Haka* isn't about the individual and Kane tells me that Māori are much more at home with the idea of group happiness than individual happiness. 'Ideas of contentment are always communal. Happiness is a shared value and if one person isn't having a good time, then the group unites to change the tone of a gathering,' Kane tells me. It's such a communal culture that even the word *māori* means 'normal', or 'ordinary' – originally used to distinguish mortals from the deities and spirits (*wairua*) in legends and oral traditions. 'Basically, we're all in it together,' says Kane, ' – and *haka* is no different. At the end, everyone can look at each other satisfied and happy.'

Thanks to the language projects, more Māori got to learn about *haka*, and with the expansion of the Māori culture education programme, younger tribal members were able regain more of their culture's birthrights. During the 1990s and 2000s, Māori people negotiated for a redress for past persecution, accepting more than NZ$900 million in settlements, often in the form of land deals. This secured and protected a physical *tūrangawaewae* for tribal members and ensured that future Māori can experience the happiness of a *tūrangawaewae*. One's *tūrangawaewae* always involves other people and it's always shared – only now Māori are ensuring that there is legal protection to stop it from being misused or taken away again.

'We're also becoming more worldly in terms of our culture and the way we represent *haka*,' says Kane. *Haka* has become something of a curiosity to the rest of the world, co-opted to sell everything from gingerbread to hatchbacks, but although as a rule Māori are generous with their heritage, they're also protective of how it's performed and represented. 'We don't accept that anyone can just appropriate our culture to use as they will,' Kane tells me, explaining that Māori people will go to great lengths to defend their *taonga*, or 'gift'. 'But the fundamental ideas shared by *haka* are universal and open for everyone to experience,' he says.

Former Māori Party co-leader Marama Fox has encouraged the teaching of *haka* in different parts of the world, arguing that it positively promotes Māori culture. It's because of this that Kane obtained the blessing of his Ngāti Kahu elders to 'open and share the pathway to that history and ancestry' and has now been sharing Māori culture throughout Europe for twenty years. And this is how I ended up saying 'yes' to the offer of giving *haka* a go.

Kane begins his *haka* workshop with a handshake where we grip each other by the right forearm creating a 'life spiral'. 'This represents our willingness to share our energy and bring it to this experience,' Kane says. Reaching forward to touch each other's shoulders with our left hand, we remind ourselves that we stand on the shoulders of our ancestors. I realise that we seldom acknowledge or reference our elders in my home culture, save for perhaps the occasional, 'Grandma would be proud' when we manage to master a Sunday roast. It's good to be reminded to be grateful for who and what brought us here. Kane goes on to explain how his goal is to 'orchestrate a type of unkempt energy a lot of people often don't know they have, then give it back to them in a way they can understand'. This is daunting. 'My mantra is that your soul will always tell an authentic story, and even if we try to hide it will always reveal itself eventually.'

My soul really wants to hide my story, but by using hands, arms, legs, feet, voice, eyes, tongue and the body as a whole in an ensemble of the unfamiliar, I find I'm experiencing something quite unlike anything I've ever felt before. As a 21st-century lady-woman, I'm not used to taking up space. I'm also not used to being loud. Or shouting. Or stamping. Or any of the things that *haka* is calling upon me to do. It's transformative, breaking me out of comfort zones I've previously cleaved to. It strikes me that *haka* is a Very Good Thing Indeed for modern women to partake in. And by the end I am spent. And in tears. And all I want to do it get home to my family – my *tūrangawaewae*. This, apparently, is the point.

'The Western world bottles up a lot of emotions,' says Kane, 'but *haka* is about letting these go with an open heart, fully taken up with the group. And a *tūrangawaewae* is what we all need, deep down.'

Now is not a time for tribalism. Or war. Or encouragement of aggression in anyone, especially men. But gratitude, honesty about our emotions and recognising where we've come from? We could all do with a bit more of that.

HOW TO FIND YOUR *TŪRANGAWAEWAE*

1

Close your eyes and imagine what you'd do if the
world ended tomorrow.

2

Who would you spend time with? Where would you go?
Now, go there and treasure that space and those people. Always.

HOW TO EXPERIENCE *HAKA*

1

Watch one online, giving yourself the time and space to let yourself
be moved (*who started cutting up onions in here?*).

2

Feeling brave? Find a *haka* near you (led by a Māori, please, to culturally
appreciate rather than culturally appropriate).

3

Take a break from bottling up your emotions. Instead,
let them go – with an open heart. Crying is optional. Getting out of
your comfort zone once in a while, isn't.

FRILUFTSLIV

F riluftsliv (pronounced 'free-lufts-liv'), noun, meaning 'free air life' or 'open-air living' – a philosophical term popularised by the Norwegian playwright Henrik Ibsen in his 1859 poem 'On The Heights' to describe the value of spending time in remote locations for spiritual and physical well-being. Now adopted by neighbouring Swedes and Danes as well, this way of life is still best exemplified by the Norwegians.

NORWAY

It's minus five degrees, it's a Monday morning, and the sun is a distant memory. I'm fumbling to procure my first coffee of the day and lamenting the fact that last night's blizzard shows no sign of abating. But my fellow breakfast buffet companions are upbeat. Model-esque Nordic super-beings stomp about, searching for pickled herring, in full ski gear, discussing how best to get a few 'runs' in before work. Neither sleet, nor snow, nor sub-par weather of any kind is going to keep them from their *friluftsliv* – and they all look sickeningly well on it. Oslo, where I find myself for work, has world-class museums, insanely impressive eateries, and – in my experience at least – a surfeit of tall, taut, Scandi demi-gods. It's not a place to visit if you're suffering from low self-esteem.

This is Norway – the two-pronged pincer of Scandinavia and the country that brought us Edvard Munch, Henrik Ibsen and a-ha. With a population of just 5.3 million, Norwegians enjoy all the benefits of the Nordic Welfare model with the added safety net of a butt load of oil, bolstering the country's finances and accounting for a quarter of Norway's GDP. In addition to this, Norway recently ousted Denmark as the UN's 'happiest country on earth' and has been ranked 'World's Best Democracy' for the past six years by The Economist Intelligence Unit's Democracy Index. But it's for the region's natural attributes that Norway is really winning.

Native species include arctic foxes, wolves, whales, basking sharks, elk ('moose', for North American readers), and polar bears – aka 'all the really cool ones' as my four-year-old puts it. Famed for mountains, glaciers and fjords – deep grooves cut into the land flooded by the sea following the end of the Ice Age – the Norwegian landscape is unequivocally spectacular. It boasts lows, like Hornindalsvatnet, the deepest lake in Europe; and permafrosted highs – peaks with fairytale-esque names like 'Glittertind' and dream-like vistas. And this is where *friluftsliv* comes in.

'It's a very big part of who we are – and how we are,' Erik Salvesen tells me in a characteristically singsong west coast voice. 'The best way to explain it is the literal translation: "free air life" – but that doesn't really cover it. You have to experience *friluftsliv* to fully understand it and how important it is for Norwegians.' Erik and I first crossed paths in 2013 when I interviewed him for the *Guardian* about the launch of the world's first ever Viking theme park in Haugesund (think 'less Disney plastic, more axe-throwing and sword skills'). He's passionate about bringing 'the good bits' of Viking culture to a wider audience – and that includes *friluftsliv*.

'Norway has a small population spread out over a large area, so wild nature is only one or two minutes away for most people – it's very accessible,' says Erik. 'Hunting and fishing have always been hugely important to Norwegians – especially in the fjord districts,' he says, and while Norwegians traditionally spent time in nature for survival, now they do it for recreation. '*Friluftsliv* helps to feed our soul,' says Erik. 'Even in big cities –' He stops to correct himself: 'Well, we only have one big city, so: "even in Oslo", most people have access to a cottage in the mountains. *Friluftsliv* is too important to do without.' He describes the experience of spending time in the great outdoors as 'spiritual', adding, '– you feel different in nature. There are different energies. The beauty can be overwhelming, but then we relax through

activity and the wonderful panoramas calm you down.' For Erik, this is active meditation ('and we are quite calm in Norway compared to other Europeans'). He likes to get out every day, but most people will embark on an adventure 'at least' two or three times a week. 'It's very sociable – you can do it with friends and family, take some food, and make a day of it. It combines nature, activity, food, good company,' Erik goes on, listing attributes that are all proven to be good for our health and well-being.

Children learn about *friluftsliv* from birth in Norway, and even once they start school, aged six, they're outside a lot. 'We have another word, *fjellvant*, which means "being accustomed to walk in the mountains",' says Erik, '– and this is very common for all ages.' Norway's *fjellvettreglene* – or 'mountain code' - encourages a respectful relationship with nature, something that is crucial to Norwegian culture. Because Norwegians, it seems, like to get high. 'Getting up high gives you an aim,' explains Erik, 'and if you meet a Norwegian out in nature, their objective tends to be the highest mountain nearby.' I tell him this sounds like hard work. 'It is. That's the point. You have to earn it. We have a saying: *Du må yte før du kan nyte*, meaning "You must make an effort before you can have pleasure". Then you get *kos* – as in the Norwegian word *koselig*, or "getting cosy", like the Danish *hygge*.'

The ultimate reward comes after the winter with *utepils* – the first beer enjoyed outdoors to celebrate the weather being, if not 'warm', then 'slightly less cold'. 'When you've longed for many months to get out into the sun – or at least the less dark – there is nothing better,' Erik muses. 'Especially in the fjords, enjoying fresh prawns...' he tails off in rapture. And when does this *'not quite so wintery as before'* day occur? 'Usually April, if you're lucky. Although it can be later... Whatever day we all agree it's time for *utepils*, there are always pictures of people drinking their first beer in the papers.' Like the long-hallowed UK press tradition of a photogenic schoolgirl opening her GCSE results, it seems all Norwegians are on the same page on this one.

In common with her Scandinavian neighbours, Norway is a country of collective experiences that unite her inhabitants. So when Norwegians aren't all celebrating with *utepils* on exactly the same day, or getting active together in the great outdoors, they're congregating around the television to get their *friluftsliv* fix vicariously.

The biggest broadcasting hit of the past decade in Norway has been Slow TV – the real-time airing of seemingly mundane events in their entirety, usually concerned with the natural world. The concept has been a hit since Norway's public service broadcaster NRK televised the view of mountains and fjords out of the window during a seven-hour train journey in 2009 – to an audience of 1.2 million. Norwegian audiences have also been treated to the vistas from a cruise ship during a five-and-a-half-day journey along the Norwegian coast, which attracted a 36 per cent share of Norway's TV viewing market. Other Slow TV successes include a twelve-hour show about a fire being built and lit; an eighteen-hour salmon fishing

special; and 168 hours of live reindeer migration. It's hardly your average blockbuster fare, but as Thomas Hellum, a producer at NRK, tells me, 'It's all about *friluftsliv*.'

I first met Thomas when Slow TV was in its infancy and no one thought it would catch on. It's now a TV staple in Norway, exported worldwide, and even has a dedicated following on Netflix. I apologise, belatedly, for doubting Thomas. He tells me I'm forgiven, and that he's feeling serene as he's just been skiing and getting his *friluftsliv* on. It is 1pm on a Tuesday. Not bad, I think. 'Slow TV works because Norwegians are all in love with nature – the mountains and the water. We see nice pictures and the scenery speaks to all of us – it feeds our soul,' says Thomas. 'There's something deep in Norwegians' roots. It's the dream of most Norwegians – and if you took *friluftsliv* away, something would disappear.' I ask him about Erik's theory whereby Norwegians are at their most delirious when there's a mountain nearby and he breaks into a grin: 'We do love to get up high. Everyone looks smaller from up there, and so do your problems. People from other countries often don't understand this.' From any countries in particular? 'Denmark,' he says, without missing a beat: 'and maybe The Netherlands. The flat ones.' There's a different approach to heights in countries that don't have any, but in Norway they are obsessed. 'People might say to us, "Why couldn't you quit twenty metres from the top? You already have a nice view..." but for a Norwegian, that's unthinkable!' Thomas shakes his head: 'There's something ingrained in

Norwegians to get out, climb a mountain, maybe ski down it a few times. We have to do this once or twice a week, and on the days we can't do it, we watch it.' His latest Slow TV show involves a group of volunteers walking in four different mountains over four weeks. 'There'll be live transmission during the day, then we'll film them building camp in the evening. The next morning, we'll broadcast them making their packed lunch and then setting off again.' It's thrilling stuff.

And where will they go?

'Anywhere!' Thomas tells me: 'That's the beauty of it. *Friluftsliv* is a right for all Norwegians. The land belongs to us all.' Since 1957 Norway has had a *Lov om friliftslivet*, or 'Outdoor Recreation Act', stating that: 'At any time of the year, outlying property may be crossed on foot, with consideration and due caution'. So everyone can roam free, even on private land, as well as pitch a tent, wake up to birdsong, and breakfast by a campfire before foraging for lunch. 'As long as you're considerate and you carry with you what you're going to eat, no one will stop you,' says Thomas. 'It's there for the taking. And it's a challenge.' This is because there's something else Norway boasts in bucketloads: weather.

'We have A Lot of weather in Norway,' Thomas admits.'It dictates your

day – whether or not you have to reschedule meetings, whether or not you can get your car on the roads. Everything. We have two seasons: "spring-summer" and "winter".' Then he corrects himself: 'Except in Bergen, where I live. There, we have "the wet one" and "the even wetter one".'

But Norwegians don't let a bit of rain/snow/sleet stop them.

'If it's too snowy to walk, you ski,' he says simply. 'We get active no matter what because you have to earn your relaxation. Most Norwegians believe you have to work for things, to earn them with physical endeavours, battling the elements. Once you've climbed a mountain in the rain and cold, then you can really enjoy your dinner,' says Thomas, who insists that food tastes better if you've climbed a mountain to earn it. 'Plus we always have a sense that the people before us, our ancestors, used their muscles and really did something. So we have to ask ourselves – What did we do today? What did we climb? Where did we go? That's a big part of *friluftsliv*. And that's happiness in Norway.'

HOW TO LIVE THE *FRILUFTSLIV* LIFE

1

Climb every mountain – summits are there to be surmounted, plus things look better with a little perspective.

2

Earn your lunch, always. Play/climb/hike/ski first: *then* relax.

3

Get out there, whatever the forecast. There's no such thing as bad weather, only the wrong clothes.

4

Slow down – be it with TV or by paying attention to the way the landscape changes with the seasons.

5

Enjoy an *utepils* – or your tipple of choice – al fresco on the first nice day of the year.

AZART

Azart, noun, meaning heat, excitement, ardour, fervour or passion – also associated with recklessness and risk-taking. From the French *hasard*, meaning 'chance'. An emotion associated with anticipating success, however realistic or likely. Often used in connection with a game or taking on something dangerous. Like love. Or a roulette table.

RUSSIA

A big country of big hats and even bigger emotions, Russia isn't renowned for its happiness. Think 'Russia' and most of us probably think of Putin; the country's Soviet past; or even its literary legacy, courtesy of Chekhov, Tolstoy, Turgenev, Dostoyevsky or Pushkin. You know, that chipper lot. Moscow was recently voted the most unfriendly city in the world and Russian children are allegedly taught not to smile at school (too busy cribbing up on Pushkin presumably…). But could we in the West have Russia pegged all wrong? Ksenia is a friend of a friend from Chelyabinsk in the Ural Mountains, and one frosty Friday she introduces me to the concept of *azart*. It's not happiness as we know it – at least not in the happy-go-lucky sense of the word – but it's a celebration of excitement, heat and most importantly, passion.

'You use *azart* to describe the feeling in the game when you can't stop yourself – on the crest of the emotional wave,' says Ksenia. 'It has an association with that rush of excitement. But it's also very relevant to happiness in Russia. We're a very emotional people and a lot of decisions are made via our emotions – eyes closed, on a wave of passion.' Because *azart* is an anticipation of the thrill: the delicious pain of teetering on the edge of something that gives many Russians a zeal for life that we can all learn from.

Mother Russia was famously described by Winston Churchill as 'a riddle wrapped in a mystery inside an enigma' or, as Ksenia puts it: 'Russia is a tough country, so we've created some unique ways of enjoying our lives.'

People have a lot of misconceptions about Russians, she tells me. 'They assume everyone is cruel, that everyone is the same as the government. But we aren't. We're damaged souls; a unique people, kind, and badly treated by the state.' There's also something fatalistic about the Russian mentality: 'We're like cockroaches, we can survive anything – and we learn to be grateful for what we have.' Many Russians have had no choice. In the Soviet Union, clothes, food, even homes, were allocated by ticket. 'Things were literally thrown to you in a crowd,' says Ksenia, 'and people would be grateful, thankful that someone had given them something. Anything. Because they had nothing. And we should therefore try to make a life with what we have.'

It's out of this landscape that an unusual kind of happiness developed – the feeling of *azart* as a heat source to be grabbed hold of whenever possible to sustain you. Russia has historically been very family-orientated, with all the patriarchy that traditionally comes with this. 'The message for girls growing up was very clearly, "Be a wife" – always have good food in the kitchen for when your man comes home: get a borscht on, go make love, have kids!"' Ksenia tells me. 'For men, it was "Get a good job, a clean house, a 'good' wife and kids."' It's the stuff of greetings cards. 'There's an old Russian phrase: "You're successful in life once you've built a house, planted a tree and had kids." And really, that was what most people aspired to,' says Ksenia. Then in the 1990s, the Soviet Union collapsed and people started wanting more. Cars, money, houses...*more*. Everyone started working young and worked as hard as they possibly could to get ahead. Ksenia explains it as being 'all about the destination', rather than enjoying the ride. And so this particular Russian idea of happiness comes not from cultivating a calm, contented, consistent feeling of happiness, but from grabbing fleeting moments of pleasure with both hands.

Azart may also have something to do with the weather (spoiler alert: it's cold) as many Russians feel compelled to seek out heat – 'both literally and in our inner lives through conversation', says Ksenia. She explains that if a Russian knocks into you in the street, they won't stop to say sorry: it's just accepted that the name of the game is to get indoors and into the warmth as quickly as possible. But, once indoors, everything heats up. Another idea I come across when researching Russian happiness is *posidelki* or 'kitchen talks' – literally, sitting around the kitchen table with friends and family talking about anything and everything. It makes sense – close relationships with friends and family along with frequency of contact and open dialogues are proven by almost every relevant study in the world to be a central component of happiness. Only in Russia, conversation gets hot and heavy, fast.

'We get straight into really deep topics,' says Ksenia. 'So while Brits are good at small talk, making polite, *bla bla bla…*' – she demonstrates this with a puppet hand and an eye roll – 'in Russia, we delve right in. With alcohol of course.' Of course. Alcohol has a dicey relationship with happiness levels, but skilfully deployed it can be key in building bonds and…well, having a really good night (see 'Ireland'). My editor is at pains for me to point out that alcohol is categorically NOT a pillar of well-being. But if it were, Russians would all be in rude health. Alcohol consumption remains among

the highest in the world and the average Russian drinks 20 litres of vodka a year, according to research from Oxford University. Drinking is so ingrained in the culture that there's a word to describes a multi-day drinking binge (*'zapoi'*) and until 2011, beer wasn't deemed strong enough to 'count' as alcoholic.

Russia's size also plays into the psyche when it comes to bonding and happiness. As well as 'kitchen talks', Ksenia enthuses about the delights of another Russian institution: 'train talks' (*razgovory v poezde*). Russia is such a big country that you can spend seven days crossing it on a train, passing through eleven different time zones. Everyone is together in cabins, sharing food and conversation – 'so someone might bring a chicken, others might bring the alcohol, and people who you don't know before the trip will all live together, eat together and talk together,' says Ksenia, 'until you step off the train the other end as friends.' This is a genial idea, but as a Brit I'm not convinced that a week trapped on a train with strangers would really be conducive to happiness.

I point this out to Ksenia, who concedes: 'Well, you do suffer a little – but then, we Russians like to suffer.' *Aha, this must be where I've been going wrong.* Ksenia adds: 'Two hours before the station in any big city, you aren't allowed to go to the toilet as it's just a drop onto the tracks – so you suffer then, too. There are no showers, either, so we take a bottle of water and pour it over ourselves, straddling the coupling between two carriages, or jump off the train before any stop near a lake to jump in. It's suffering, but we like this. We are charged with *azart* – it's a part of us.'

Non-essential suffering – like ticking off a to-do list – gives us a dopamine hit and makes us feel we have achieved something, but I can't help feeling that Russians are taking this to another level. When Ksenia's countryfolk arrive at their destination, many find another way of suffering and seeking heat – in a Russian sauna, or *banya*. Many Russians consider *banya* a crucial ingredient for a happy life and it's a part of the weekly routine: some go every Sunday to prepare for the week ahead, and workers even have *banya* meetings held at 100 °C. Living in Scandinavia, I've had a fair few sauna experiences – but the Russian version appears to embrace the 'suffering' element as standard. As well as getting their sweat on, Russians eat and drink in their saunas (often 'heavily'), then 'vigorously beat themselves with birch twigs, before going outside to cover themselves with snow'. (see 'suffering')

'Visitors often exclaim in horror at this, demanding, "Why do you want to beat yourself up then get cold?",' Ksenia says, 'But it's a cultural thing. It comes from our history and our religion. You had to stand during mass where I grew up – there were no seats, and you spend the whole night in church at Christmas and Easter. My granny is eighty years old and she still walks for forty minutes to go to church twice a week because she wants to suffer to deserve what she has. At Easter, when Jesus walked with a cross, she felt she needed to as well. On her way to church with this big cross, she fell and broke her leg. I said to her, "Granny, maybe this wasn't such a good idea..." But she told me: "No! It is because I had a bad thought during my walk and so this is God's punishment...this is good. I have suffered, now I can be happy."' This throws shade on the hardships of weak tea and bad biscuits in a draughty church hall in the Home Counties. But it gets to the core of what it is that keeps people going, in the dead of winter, in six-foot snow drifts, or just in times of great hardship. The human spirit is strong. And maybe – just maybe – we all have this heat, this fire, this *azart* inside us. By talking deeply, drinking freely [Ed: this is non-compulsory], and grabbing onto everything life throws at us, perhaps our *azart* can sustain us, helping us to make it through our suffering, deserving of the happiness to come.

HOW TO EXPERIENCE *AZART*

1

Take a risk: roll those dice. Many of us are prone to damage limitation and caution, but while risk-taking is scary, it's also exciting – and excitement is happiness-inducing.

2

Try skipping the small talk: have dangerously deep, impassioned, possibly vodka-fuelled conversations around the kitchen table next time someone comes round for dinner.

3

Make like the Russians and suffer a little for your next dopamine hit. Go for a walk on a freezing cold day, throw yourself into a gruelling task that you've been putting off forever, or find your nearest sauna (birch twigs and snow-rolling optional). You'll enjoy whatever post-self-flagellation treat you choose so much more.

UBUNTU

Ubuntu (pronounced 'ooh-boon-to'), noun, in Bantu languages, from *-ntú*, meaning 'human being' and *ubu* – a prefix to form the abstract noun 'humanity'. A term in use since the 19th century that means, 'I find my worth in you and you find your worth in me'; a sense of interconnection and the belief in a universal bond of sharing that connects all humanity. Bantu is spoken by Bantu peoples spanning Central Africa, Southern Africa and the African Great Lakes region, but the concept of *ubuntu* has been claimed by South Africa in the past thirty years as a humanitarian objective to live by.

SOUTH AFRICA

It's 2013 and the memorial service for Nelson Mandela is being broadcast on television screens worldwide. Barack Obama is giving a eulogy in Soweto, Johannesburg, and halfway through his stirring tribute, he says: 'There is a word in South Africa – *ubuntu* – that describes his [Mandela's] greatest gift: his recognition that we are all bound together in ways that can be invisible to the eye; that there is a oneness to humanity; that we achieve ourselves by sharing ourselves with others, and caring for those around us.' This was the first time I had ever heard the term *ubuntu* – having been too young to fully appreciate its significance during the anti-apartheid movement. But it struck me. And I became, for a while, mildly obsessed.

'So you should have been,' Vusi, a friend of a friend from Welkom in the Free State province tells me. '*Ubuntu* is an ethical approach to life that's crucial for happiness. It's about feeling interconnected – living in peace and harmony with others – and it's the essence of humanity.' Big claim, Vusi, big claim... 'But it's true,' he tells me, 'because how can you be happy if the people around you aren't?' He's got a point. *Ubuntu* is a philosophical term but it's also strongly linked to traditional community values. 'And it's who we are as South Africans,' says Vusi.

The concept was first documented in 1846 as a way to express the need to restore dignity to the people of Africa after the cruelties of colonisation. *Ubuntu* later became a term used by South Africans to assert their own identity and values in opposition to previously imposed colonial ones. The concept was popularised in the 1950s, via the writings of Jordan Kush Ngubane in *The African Drum* (now *Drum* magazine) and by the 1970s, *ubuntu* was shorthand for a special kind of African humanism. In the 1990s, *ubuntu* went global as a guiding light for the anti-apartheid movement and even appears in South Africa's Interim Constitution, created in 1993. When Nelson Mandela became the country's first black president in 1994, set on tackling institutionalised racism and fostering reconciliation, the notion of 'I am because you are' looked set to define modern South Africa. Archbishop Desmond Tutu promoted *ubuntu* as a theological concept that drove his work as chairman of the South African Truth and Reconciliation Commission. In an interview about his 2004 book, *God Has A Dream*, he told Dr Frank Lipman: '*Ubuntu* is the essence of being a person. It means that we are people through other people. We can't be fully human alone. We are made for interdependence, we are made for family. Indeed, my humanity is caught up in your humanity, and when your humanity is enhanced mine is enhanced as well. Likewise, when you are dehumanised, inexorably, I am dehumanised as well.'

Ubuntu is about placing a high value on the life and well-being of another human being. It means 'compassion' and 'respect', says Vusi, and today it's viewed as an ethical tenet that promotes mutual understanding and generosity. All of us have a collective responsibility with *ubuntu* and a community is advanced through recognition and appreciation of individual difference – not in spite of it. So whereas sceptics of socialism fear that compulsory sharing makes everybody worse off in the long run,

ubuntu proposes that helping those around us simultaneously improves our lot – as well as society as a whole. 'It's inclusive and embracing,' says Vusi, 'and it's probably the most important lesson I live my life by.'

But aren't we always being told not to take all the troubles of the world on our shoulders? Won't we suffer from compassion fatigue if we care too much, about everyone? 'No,' is the answer: 'Because "everyone" is your family,' says Vusi, 'they make you, you.' He doesn't mean this literally, rather that our connection to humanity is 'always wider than our blood ties.' *Ubuntu* means saying to the people around us: 'I understand your struggle. I appreciate your journey.' And we're all on a journey of one kind or another.

Nelson Mandela's autobiography *Long Walk to Freedom* documented his twenty-seven years in prison on Robben Island. He had more cause than most of us to be pretty hacked off with the world, and disinclined to take on any more of its pain or its problems. But that was never an option for Mandela, because of *ubuntu*. In 2006, the South

African journalist Tim Modise interviewed Mandela and asked how he would define the concept, to which Mandela replied: 'In the old days when we were young, a traveller through a country would stop at a village, and he didn't have to ask for food or water; once he stops, the people give him food, entertain him. That is one aspect of *ubuntu*.' *Ubuntu* doesn't mean that we shouldn't look after ourselves, rather that we also have an obligation to 'enable the community' around us and so 'enable it to improve', as Mandela put it. By this measure, *ubuntu* is the promise of an open society and a sustainable future for all.

That's not to say *ubuntu* can always be seen in action in South Africa today. Inequality is rife, corruption is widespread and, as Vusi says, 'South Africa is still not a happy country.' *Ubuntu* can be challenged by modern life and as Vusi warns: 'We're often told by the media that in order to be happy we need more money, or to look a certain way or dress a certain way – we live in a world of iPhones and the internet and people focus on "stuff". But this isn't *ubuntu* – and wanting more "stuff" only makes us unhappy in the long run.' Jay Naidoo, a former minister in Mandela's cabinet turned political and social activist, argues in his book *Change: Organising Tomorrow, Today* that: 'We need to retrace our steps and build the spirit of *ubuntu*. I appeal for a return to the values that made us a political miracle in 1994.' He told South Africa's *News 24* in 2017: 'We have to co-create a new future in which we have humanity, love, and compassion. We cannot only write about , we must live it.'

So don't just read about *ubuntu*: live it.

Feel for your fellow man or woman, no matter where they are from, what they do for a living, or how much 'stuff' they have. As Vusi puts it: 'We have to harness *ubuntu* to go beyond our individual limitations and to be able to challenge whatever boundaries are thrown our way.'

HOW TO LIVE AN *UBUNTU* LIFE

1

Forgive. Yes, this is hard. Often painfully so.
But it's almost always the best way to make progress.

2

Appreciate your journey. It may not be as dramatic or noble as some but
it's yours – and owning it can help you move forward.

3

Cherish the people who make you *you*. And remember: family isn't just
about blood ties. Open yourself up to humanity at large.

4

Care more. Even about people you don't know. Even when it hurts
to look at the pictures of despair and desperation in the newspapers.
Because that's life. As Desmond Tutu said: 'I am sorry to say
that suffering is not optional.'

5

Ditch Descartes' 'I think therefore I am' (now there's a sentence
I never thought I'd write) – it's time for a new philosophical bumper
sticker: 'I am because you are.'

TAPEO & SOBREMESA

Tapeo, (pronounced 'tap-ay-oh'), verb, from the noun *tapas* and the suffix *eo*, informal slang for meeting friends in the street to walk together to a bar for a drink and something to eat – a holy tradition in Spain and the definition of happiness for many.

Sobremesa, (pronounced 'sob-rem-essa'), noun, from *sobre* meaning 'over' and *mesa*, meaning 'table', *sobremesa* means 'over the table' talks. Used to describe the period of time after a meal when the food is finished but conversation is still flowing.

SPAIN

Imagine an evening so warm that you're out without a coat (inconceivable for many of us, I know. Still: stick with it...). The sun's dipped below the horizon but the cobbled streets give off a welcome heat and there's a flicker of anticipation; a feeling in the air that the night ahead exists only for pleasure. Now imagine that a few of your favourite people have appeared and you're walking together, with the sole aim of procuring snacks and refreshments of some kind. Perhaps you'll have a glass of wine; maybe a martini; probably some *calamares*. You'll talk and eat and drink and then move on to another bar to do the same again. And again. And again – until you decide to call it a night, safe in the knowledge that a good time has been had by all. Now doesn't that sound tempting? This is *ir de tapeo* – and this is Spanish happiness.

'*Tapeo* is everything in Spain – wherever you are,' Diego, a graphic designer from Andalusia, tells me. 'Even if you live in the countryside, you'll get a bus from your village every Saturday night.' 'Life without *tapeo* is unimaginable,' my friend Marta from San Sebastian confirms. 'You might go out on a Saturday and start at 7.30 p.m., then see where the night takes you.' *Ir de tapeo* ('going for tapas') usually involves an alcoholic beverage in one hand and snacks in the other with both consumed standing up, either at the bar or on the street. Spaniards chat, eat, drink, then walk to the next bar and repeat the process until 'at least three' establishments, and 'possibly seven or so...' have been patronised, Marta tells me.

'If you're in your twenties you'll be out until around 11 a.m. the next day when it's time to go for some *churros* dipped in chocolate sauce,' says Diego. Diego is in his twenties. 'Then, if you're in your thirties,' – he near shudders at the thought – 'it can be 5 a.m. or 7 a.m. – and in your forties, *maybe* 2 a.m. But no earlier!' *Don't you feel like death the next day?* 'Sure you do!' he tells me, but apparently this is fine because you know you're going to feel bad so you don't make plans. The Spanish don't do brunch. 'We're like "What is this? It's the weekend! Why are you up before noon?" No. Just "no".' Instead, *tapeo*-fatigued Spaniards may have breakfast at 1 p.m. followed by a light lunch at 3 p.m. before starting all over again.

'There's no socialising without food or drink in Spain,' says Marta, 'and in every place you eat something small, so after a few hours, you've basically had a whole meal.' In many bars, the tapas come free when you buy a drink. 'There's often no space to sit,' says Marta, 'so you'll be like sardines in a can, but because you're standing it feels more dynamic – you can mingle and socialise more freely.' Numerous studies show that standing is preferable to sitting from a health perspective and a report from the Mayo Clinic found that being on your feet for six hours a day can even reduce the risk of obesity by a third. OK, so necking sangria simultaneously might counteract some of the benefits, but imbibing in an upright position has to be better than slumped in a chair, right? *Right?* 'I don't know about that,' Marta frowns, reminding me that she's a designer, not a doctor, 'but there's definitely something about socialising outside, standing up, that makes you feel alive.' And Spain's favourable climate is conducive to spending time out of doors.

The sun shines much of the year around in Spain, giving its 46.5 million inhabitants a repeat prescription of mood-boosting vitamin D, and there's no need to hibernate during a Spanish winter. Even during the cooler months, Spaniards get their *tapeo* fix, which is great because regular contact with friends, as well as spending time outdoors, has been proven to be good for mental health. Marta agrees that the communal aspect of *tapeo* is key to its appeal: 'There's a real buzz from just being around other people,' she tells me, 'it's like we're all enjoying a collective experience. Together.' Diego agrees: 'Just going out onto the street and seeing people having a good time makes you happy – even if you don't know them, the noise and the cheerfulness is contagious!'

The Spanish like to do things together. They also like to vent. 'There's nothing like a good night out and a moan,' says Marta, '– and venting makes us happy.' Twentieth-century philosopher and fellow Basque, Miguel de Unamuno, believed that complaining helped us to commune with our fellow man/woman and wrote in his essay 'My Religion': 'Whenever I have felt a pain I have shouted and I have done it publicly' to 'start the grieving chords of others' hearts playing.' Research from the University of Melbourne has also found that complaining can be cathartic – something Marta and her mates have always just known instinctively. 'We really like to moan about money – so taxes or our salary or having no cash to last until the end of the month. Spain often scores low on the happiness ratings and we've had plenty of political problems, too...' she tells me, waving a hand that I take to summarise everything from the Spanish Civil War and Franco to The Great Recession that started in 2008 and lasted for almost a decade. 'We have a lot of material to work with,' she tells me, 'but in some ways we like the drama.' In common with most Latin cultures, the Spanish possess a natural extroversion that can baffle northern Europeans or Asians. 'We like to share about our private life,' says Marta, 'and nothing is held back. Huge dramas are normal here. The support you get from friends feels like a sense of relief, so if you don't share, you don't get that relief. We want to experience these intense feelings and express ourselves – it's almost a source of pride,' she tells me, adding: 'There is life as long as there is passion.' *All right, Lorca...* 'Sharing our dramas, drinking and eating,' she says, 'that's happiness in Spain. But mostly the food...' Marta is a slip of a thing but her meal-mantra has long been: *'Eat until there is no room in your trousers. Then undo the top button and keep on going.'*

Marta is an inspiration.

Food is fundamental to living the good life in Spain and Marta tells me how every region takes pride in its own speciality: 'You can get the best seafood in Galicia and the best paella in Valencia.' In Andalusia, they love fish so much they even have bait vending machines (as my friend Gen from Australia put it: 'If you've ever seen one of those before let minnow'). 'You can also get the best *gazpacho* in Andalusia and we're really famous for *pintxos* in the Basque country,' says Marta. Another distinguishing feature of Basque culture is the phenomenon of *txokos*, or gastronomical societies, food clubs where people gather to cook and enjoy their own food. 'It's fun to talk to people as you cook and eat communally, alongside other families or groups of friends,' Marta tells me. But it's also a massive undertaking. 'If you're hosting, you have to make sure there's enough food for a hundred people even if there are only five of you,' says Marta. A good rule of thumb is that you 'shouldn't be able to see the table underneath all the food'. This can take time. 'You might spend ten hours cooking,' Marta says, 'but afterwards you can just relax and sit around, chatting.'

The Spanish have a word that specifically refers to the conversations that take place post food: *sobremesa*. Often linked to the idea of being too full to move, *sobremesa* is akin to being pinned down in your chair by the sheer weight of your own stomach. This not-unpleasant sensation means that you have no option but to surrender to woozy, relaxed, carb-induced conversations with the people you've broken bread with. The idea of a good life without *sobremesa* is unthinkable to most Spaniards and the experience can last anything from twenty minutes to several hours. 'If you meet someone at 3 o'clock for lunch, then you know you can't meet anyone else until at least 8 p.m.,' says Marta. Because: *sobremesa*. 'It's pure pleasure,' she tells me, 'It's a way to show your appreciation for all the food that someone has made you.' Meals can be multi-generational affairs in Spain with children welcome at restaurants and most social gatherings. Hunger is no prerequisite and Marta tells me about another superb word in the Spanish lexicon: *gula*. This is the desire to eat simply for the taste – a sensation every self-confessed glutton can identify with but one that is sadly underrepresented in the English dictionary.

Happiness in Spain is combining socialising with food: standing up with food or sitting down with food; they don't mind as long as there's plenty of it and they're in good company. As Marta says, 'Spaniards enjoy life – because we know how to eat.'

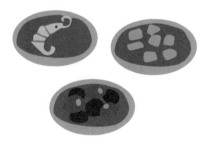

HOW TO SAMPLE *TAPEO*

1

No tapas culture in your town? Suggest that your local drinking establishment expands its edible offerings or graze at every friend's flat you can reach on foot.

2

Get a gang to join you. *Tapeo* is no time for solo introspection: get snacks, get pals, eat, drink and be merry.

3

Go out. Live in a cold country? Wrap up in so many layers you threaten to sweat and convince yourself you're somewhere hot (I call this 'a dry bath').

4

Don't fall at the first hurdle. If you're not having fun after bar number one, keep the faith: bar #6 may hold untold delights...

HOW TO EXPERIENCE *SOBREMESA*

1

Ignore everything your mother taught you and don't leap to your feet once the food's over to clear plates: sit still and see what happens.

2

If your dining companions are still inclined to spring up post-meal, encourage everyone to eat more and pour the wine until they're pinned down by their own stomachs.
Then let the philosophical musings commence...

SMULTRONSTÄLLE & LAGOM

Smultronställe (pronounced 'smul-tron-stelle'), noun, originally meaning 'wild strawberry patch' (from the Swedish words *smultron* meaning 'wild strawberries', and *ställe*, meaning 'place'). In use since the early 20th century, *smultronställe* became synonymous with a bucolic retreat where one could go to escape the world. Now used to describe a quiet place to retreat or relax; your favourite space where you can go to forget your troubles. Often somewhere that isn't easy for others to find.

Lagom (pronounced 'lah-gom'), adverb or adjective, from the Swedish word *lag* or 'team'. According to folklore, *laget om*, or 'around the team', was a phrase used by Vikings when a horn full of mead was passed around so that everyone got their fair share – not too much and not too little. Contracted to *lagom* in modern use, the meaning remained the same: 'just enough'.

SWEDEN

 Picture a place where you can go and nobody will know you're there – or, if they do, they'll know not to bother you. It's a place you can go to when you're stressed or tired or overwhelmed. It is your happy place. A shady grove, perhaps; or a quiet spot in a nearby park; a favourite café or even your own back garden. It is an underrated, low-key gem of a place, often with sentimental value, that just makes you feel better. This is your *smultronställe*.

'*Smultronställe* has a very special meaning to Swedes,' says Hanna, originally from a village just outside Malmö. 'Everyone has one and it's different from person to person. It's my favourite place where I go when I need to get energy.' Sweden is a famously 'happy' country of egalitarian ideals that regularly tops the polls for contentedness worldwide. So could a *lagom* approach to life with the guarantee of your own personal *smultronställe* help enhance Swedish happiness? Hanna thinks so.

Many Swedes first encounter the idea of *smultronställe* from Elsa Beskow's classic children's book, *Children of the Forest*, published in 1910 and illustrated with flaxen-haired infants skewering wild strawberries onto a blade of thick, straw-like grass (called *timotei*, but not to be mistaken for the popular British shampoo brand). The 'Children of the Forest' live deep in the roots of an old pine tree and occupy their days playing with squirrels, collecting wild berries, and sheltering under toadstools when it rains. 'I can picture it now,' says Hanna. 'Those images you grow up with never quite leave you. And it's something that all Swedish children do in summer,' she tells me, 'you fill your straw – your thick blade of grass – up with wild strawberries, then you eat them. I do this with my own kids now – it's a reminder of more carefree times'. This comforting idyll that takes you back to your youth is so entrenched in the Swedish consciousness that Ingmar Bergman made a film entitled *Smultronstället* in 1957 about a man who opened a door to find everything just as it was in his childhood.

As well as a nostalgia trip, your *smultronställe* should be an escape from the world. 'My *smultronställe* is a little glade in the middle of the nearby forest where in autumn I know I can always find chanterelle mushrooms,' says Christian, from Uppsala, who also tells me that many Swedes feel a yearning for the solitary and so pick a *smultronställe* where there's unlikely to be anyone else around. 'We find happiness with fewer people and we don't mind loneliness so much – we just think "how wonderfully silent!"' says Christian. 'We like to be alone,' Hanna agrees. 'In general I think we Swedes are more private and less vocal about our feelings. It can even seem as though we're not so happy, but we just don't tend to shout about it.' From working with Swedes and spending time in the country for business and pleasure, I've observed a degree of melancholy to the national character that seems entirely tolerable, desirable, even. As though making time for pensive self-reflection is an essential part of being human, and we shouldn't fight it. In Sweden, as in Norway, the hardships make the pleasures all the more worthwhile. And most Swedes are content with their lot – or rather, their 'just enough'.

I'm writing this from a hotel on Gotland, off the coast of Stockholm, that claims to be four stars. It is clean, it is serviceable, but it isn't anything approaching 'luxury'. There is a bed. There is rye bread for breakfast. And there is a shower. But that's it. The rest is functional minimalism of the kind that I've come to expect from the country that brought the world *lagom*.

'*Lagom* is the way most Swedes see life,' says Christian, who learned about the concept from a very young age. 'Some of my first memories from childhood are being asked, "How much food do you want?" and answering "*Lagom*." Or "Have you eaten enough?" "I've had *lagom*." Or "Do these new clothes fit you?" "Yes, they are *lagom* big." *Lagom* means 'sufficient', 'enough', 'as much or as long as it takes' and as such, the term exemplifies the Swedish outlook on life. Christian refers to Jante Law – the ten rules for living Scandi-style (see 'Denmark') and tells me: 'We grow up believing it's wrong to boast about yourself. It's even wrong to wear clothes that make you stand out too much...' I look down at my ruffle-sleeved 'statement' jumper and try to flop my hair over my outsized earrings. 'We don't like things too noisy,' he says, in a voice so soft that makes me take mine down a decibel, 'and taking up room is frowned upon in Sweden. We're not...' – he stops himself from saying 'Americans' and tries instead: '– we don't run up to people we don't know and just...' here he mimes jazz hands, then looks embarrassed at his own demonstrativeness, as if he's just invaded my personal space by even approximating a more extroverted nation. 'What I mean is, even the Danes are more outgoing than us. And the Norwegians! With their skiing...and merriness...' He says this as though it's a bad thing. 'It's like there's a sliding scale in Scandinavia from outgoing to introvert, with Norway down at the outgoing end, then the Danes, then the Swedes somewhere in the middle, then the Finns at the other end,' says Christian. 'Finns are beyond *lagom*,' he says, 'they don't necessarily talk to people. We joke: "at least we say *skål* [cheers] in Sweden – the Finns just drink".' I love an affectionate Nordic in-joke. 'But what we all have in common is a love of nature,' he says.

Just as *smultronställe* speaks of a deep appreciation for the natural world and a sense of the calm and restoration many Swedes find there, the Swedish language is littered with wonderfully evocative words used to describe various aspects of outdoor life. There's *gökotta* or 'early-morning cuckoo', meaning to wake up early enough to hear the first birds sing, and my favourite: the poetic *daggfrisk* meaning 'dew fresh' or the kind of pure, clean  feeling one might have from waking refreshed in the early morning at sunrise. As soon as the weather turns and the mercury stops hovering around the minus mark, Swedes get outside for running, hiking, or cross-country skiing followed by al fresco dining in one of the many communal barbecue pits or picnic sites. Scandinavian countries all have similar laws that allow people to walk or camp anywhere, as long as they show respect for the surrounding nature, wildlife and locals, and Sweden is no exception. More than 80 per cent of the population lives within 8 km of a national park, nature reserve or conservation area, and studies show that spending time in nature reduces stress, boosts mental health and even lowers blood pressure, according to research from NYU Langone Medical Center in New York. Swedes learn to appreciate nature from an early age, with many five-year-olds attending Saturday 'nature school' and older children learning basic foraging and map-reading skills.

'The Swedish approach to food is all about seasonal, local and organic,' says Uppsala-based food writer Liselotte, who adds: 'We love to forage. It's totally normal to spot a family in the woods with plastic buckets picking berries and mushrooms, and there are a few classic dishes that most

Swedes have in their post-foraging repertoire, such as nettle soup with boiled egg halves and blueberry pie.' According to Statistics Sweden, more than half of the population has access to a summerhouse or countryside cabin, and there's a strong drive to get back to nature and enjoy spending time outdoors – especially when it comes to exercise. Swedes will run in the rain or sleet or freezing fog and on my last visit I watched hoards of joggers hit the streets in a snowstorm, before breakfast. Each year in Skellefteå, they hold the Scandinavian Winter Bathing Championship where brave souls swim in 0.3°C water wearing nothing but their swimmers and a hat (mandatory for fear of hypothermia). Many Swedish firms encourage employees to block out chunks of their calendar to get active outdoors and the government gives companies tax breaks for promoting exercise. And then, when the cold and dark and lack of sunshine in winter finally becomes dispiriting, Swedes retreat to their homes and get *mys*. And if *smultronställe* is an escape that's often linked to being outside, then *mys* is the comfort of getting back indoors again.

'*Mys* – or cosiness – is candles, sofas and talking, mainly,' says Christian. 'We also have *fredagsmys*, or "cosy Fridays" where we eat something a bit special, by candlelight. And probably alone.' *Right... And what might that be?* 'Well, often it's potato chips.' *As in crisps? As a 'special treat'?* He nods. I tell him this seems pretty low rent. 'It's *lagom*,' he corrects me. Finger food and snacks are considered a 'treat' because no one has to cook and you're not left with a pile of dirty pots and pans, apparently. Since Swedes are exercising their socks off and eating a rainbow of foraged, locally sourced, seasonal delights the rest of the time (probably) crisps on a Friday make a nice change. 'The point is you're getting *mys* at home,' says Christian, 'and home is very important to Swedes. We have a saying: "Away is good but home is best."' Dorothy can sleep easy, but

I get his point. Despite their best outdoorsy efforts, many Swedes are faced with twenty-four hours of darkness in winter combined with sub-zero temperatures that force them to spend a lot of time inside. Homes become havens in Sweden – so it's little wonder design is such a big deal. Ikea aside, the Swedish aesthetic is acclaimed – from furniture to fashion and even fonts. In 2014 stylish Swedes decided to under-haul their branding by creating their own national typeface named 'Sweden Sans' (could there be a more *lagom* name?). Swedish government ministries, agencies and corporations wanted a clear visual brand identity that said 'Sweden' – so they took away all the bells and whistles and what was left was *lagom* Sweden Sans.

The only thing Swedes can never have enough of is coffee. Swedes are amongst the biggest coffee drinkers in the world (beaten by only the Dutch and the Finns...go figure...) and drink so much of the black stuff that they had to come up with *tretår* – a Swedish word for a 'second refill' or 'threefill'. 'This is all part of *fika*,' says Hanna, ' – similar to *hygge* but we don't feel the need to talk about it all the time like the Danes. We just do it.' *Fika* is for when Swedes have grazed their fill of isolation and are ready to get together for a chat, coffee and cake. *Fika* without cake is incomprehensible (believe me, I've asked and been met by Paddington stares countrywide) and according to the Swedish Board of Agriculture and Statistics the average Swede eats an equivalent of 316 cinnamon buns a year (but don't they look good on it?). An important aspect of *fika*

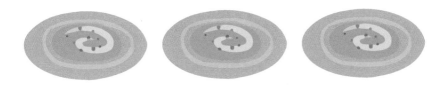

is that nobody dares take the last slice of cake or cinnamon bun. 'You could cut the last piece in half and take one half,' says Christian, quite seriously, 'then you can halve that remaining piece again. And again. And again – down to the very last crumb.' *Why?* I can't help asking. 'Because taking the last bit so that there's nothing left for others would not be *lagom*. It is something you just don't do!' Sharing and cake: both so important in Sweden that there's an entire code of conduct devoted to them.

Christian tells me that for most Swedes, the good life is about the little things – and just enough of them (except for coffee, when the *tretår* the merrier). *Lagom* is something I've been working on since moving to Scandinavia in 2013. And I think I'm getting better at it. So my house is *lagom*. My car is *lagom*. Even the six-year-old jumper I'm currently wearing that's bobbling around the elbows but is still wonderfully warm is *lagom*. And if I start to feel out of whack and need to rest, restore and recalibrate, then there's always my *smultronställe*. And cinnamon buns. And coffee.

HOW TO RESTORE YOURSELF
WITH A *SMULTRONSTÄLLE*

1

Find your symbolic strawberry patch. For me, it's the crest of a hill near my house (the only hill in Denmark...) or the back of my walk-in wardrobe where I've strung up fairy lights and can hide behind winter coats in my own personal Narnia. These are the places I go to if I've had a tough day or when I need to hide from my family (unless they're reading this, in which case, I'm just putting away clothes really thoroughly. Or taking the bins out. Back in a sec...).

2

Escape. Whenever you can. Preferably before you reach breaking point. Sit, breathe and reminisce about happy times playing with squirrels, collecting wild berries, and sheltering under toadstools when it rains.

HOW TO EXPERIENCE *LAGOM*

1

Think WWASD? (What Would A Swede Do?) – is your cup really half-empty or is there, in fact, just enough?

2

Step off the treadmill: working more to buy more is a fool's game. Think about what you optimally need (not 'want') and aim for that instead.

3

Still feeling dissatisfied with your lot? Eat cake, just not too much (sorry) and remember to share it with others. Down to the very last crumb.

FEDERERISM

Federerism* (noun), a distinctive philosophy and ideology named after the tennis player Roger Federer but indicative of the Swiss nation as a whole . A term coined to express control; precision; athleticism; industriousness; order; cleanliness – qualities embodied by the Basel-born tennis pro and shared by his country folk at large.

* I am well aware that Federerism isn't a word that appears in the dictionary *yet* but it's my book and I'll appropriate a term used by fans of the tennis player to sum up an entire nation if I want to (as the Lesley Gore song doesn't go).

SWITZERLAND

The land of Lindt balls, banking, timepieces and – lately – Tina Turner, Switzerland has frequently been named the world's happiest country in surveys spanning decades. But no one's quite sure why – least of all the Swiss. A landlocked, mountainous country with four languages, twenty-six cantons and 7.8 million people, Switzerland is responsible for bringing the world such life-changing inventions as Velcro, muesli and Toilet Duck. It's also produced twenty-five Nobel laureates and the biggest grand slam tennis champion in history. Step forward Roger Federer: man, muse and the quintessence of all that is great about Switzerland.

'We're proud of Federer in Switzerland, of course, but we don't boast about it. In fact we don't boast about anything,' says Stephan, a friend of a friend from Zurich. We speak one wintry Tuesday when I'm battling bronchitis and struggling to slough off sleep, sickness and the feeling I'm being judged. My shambolic Britishness is magnified by Stephan's cool, calm oh-so Swiss persona and he seems so 'together' that I suddenly come over all Hugh Grant in *Four Weddings* fop-mode. 'We're very rational in Switzerland,' he tells me in case I hadn't already realised: 'We have security, stability, open discussions and a good average of everything.' He tells me about how unemployment is low, taxes are low, but the quality of healthcare and 'life in general' is high.

'Plus we have the mountains,' he adds. 'And it's clean in Switzerland. Things work. We have good democracy and we are relatively well off...' That's one way of putting it. Another way is to note that Switzerland is currently eighth in the world rankings when it comes to GDP per capita and Swiss bank accounts are legendary. 'We are *content*,' is all Stephan will be drawn on when it comes to his country's deep pockets. But then, talking about the green stuff is decidedly gauche and the Swiss don't flaunt their wealth. 'Instead, they're quietly confident,' Diccon Bewes, a fellow writer and author of *Swiss Watching*, who's lived in Bern for the past thirteen years, tells me. 'There's nothing flash about them and showing off is frowned upon. They know they have a very good quality of life relative to the rest of the world – especially when they look at the UK or the USA,' says Diccon. 'There is a high level of life satisfaction in Switzerland – and deservedly so.' As a nation, the Swiss excel at preparation, order, control, consistency and the ability to be present and reap the rewards of their work. They practise, as fans of the tennis star worldwide call it, 'Federerism'.

Whether or not you're interested in sport (and for the record I'm not: run after a ball, don't run after a ball, it's all the same to me) there can be little dispute that Roger Federer is a class act. Quite aside from his excellent hair and admirable devotion to a mandigan, he is preternaturally calm on court: grunt-free, and mercifully immune to the macho strutting indulged in by the majority of male players. He is also wonderfully well-mannered and a sound recordist who worked with 'Roger' recently tells me that the star shook everyone by the hand, maintained eye contact

throughout and made sure to thank the crew after filming wrapped ('very rare'). 'He also wore the softest, highest quality woollen ware I've ever seen and smelled really, *really* good...' my spy tells me. Everyone who meets Federer comments on his equable demeanour, politeness and professionalism, with a fair few mentioning his smell, too. Similarly, the Swiss in general eschew drama in favour of decorum (and often smell nice too, in my experience). 'They're typically polite and low-key,' says Diccon. 'It can be minus seventeen degrees outside but a Swiss person will just say, "it's a little chilly" or they won't mention it at all.' The flipside of this is that the Swiss can be overly reticent. 'I used to manage a bookshop and getting anyone to tell me about their achievements in staff appraisals was a total nightmare,' says Diccon. Because 'Federerism' is about understatement.

For long periods, R-Fed operated without a coach telling him what to do and *still* won Grand Slams. His former coach Paul Annacone told press that he doubted his departure would have any impact on the master's game because 'greatness doesn't stop' – and the star excelled at being his own boss.

'Federerism' means control and the Swiss like to be in charge. Switzerland is the closest any nation has come to a direct democracy, with ordinary citizens able to propose constitutional changes and referenda available on request for any new law. The government is a permanent coalition of four parties, but no politicians can exact change without public agreement and Switzerland's twenty-six cantons are relatively autonomous. 'Something like Britain's EU referendum couldn't have just been called by one person in Switzerland,' Diccon tells me, 'because in Switzerland, the people would have to decide whether or not there

should be a referendum, then they would all have to vote on it, then they could decide whether or not to have another referendum.' Direct democracy means that the government and parliament only make about 80 per cent of the decisions and everyone is involved in the political process. This can

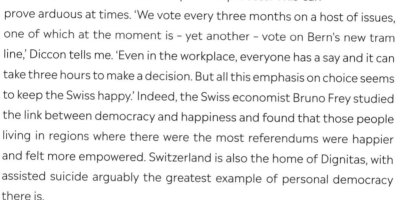

prove arduous at times. 'We vote every three months on a host of issues, one of which at the moment is – yet another – vote on Bern's new tram line,' Diccon tells me. 'Even in the workplace, everyone has a say and it can take three hours to make a decision. But all this emphasis on choice seems to keep the Swiss happy.' Indeed, the Swiss economist Bruno Frey studied the link between democracy and happiness and found that those people living in regions where there were the most referendums were happier and felt more empowered. Switzerland is also the home of Dignitas, with assisted suicide arguably the greatest example of personal democracy there is.

And then there's the cocoa. Swiss chocolate is celebrated the world over and some have speculated that perhaps tryptophan, a chemical found in chocolate that causes the release of serotonin in the brain, might be responsible for Switzerland's high happiness ratings. Even elite sports professionals in Switzerland eat the stuff, with Federer telling a journalist at last year's Australian Open: 'I like my chocolate...I like my treats, I don't feel bad about it.' But according to 'science' you'd need to eat several kilograms of chocolate to get enough tryptophan for a serotonin-stimulated mood-boost and although the country has the highest sales of chocolate in the world, a large proportion of this is exported. So forget Lindt balls: it's back to the yellow fuzzy kind. Roger's, in fact.

Roger Federer was already winning Grand Slams when he decided to work on his backhand at the age of thirty-five. He was already winning (at life...), but wanted to strive for a new, personal best – settling only for perfection. Encouraging others to adopt this work ethic, he has said: 'There's no way around hard work. Embrace it'. Other gems for your motivational mugs include: 'You have to put in a lot of sacrifice and effort for sometimes little reward but you have to know that if you put in the right effort the reward will come,' and 'When you're good at something, make that everything.' Just as Federer refuses to rest on his laurels or become complacent, the Swiss like to prepare for every eventuality. As well as being great at army knives, they also have compulsory military service for all able-bodied male citizens and run tank drills in case of attack – despite the fact that Switzerland is notoriously neutral and hasn't been involved in a war since 1847. 'Federerism' is about being meticulousness: take Swiss watches, for example, which are a masterclass in precision. Switzerland is also famed for its clean air, spotless streets and punctuality. 'This isn't just a cliché,' Diccon tells me. 'In the UK trains are considered late if they're more than ten minutes late, in Switzerland it's three minutes. And they're still on time 88 per cent of the time.' Because when you're Switzerland or Roger Federer, you aim high.

'Federerism' means being alert at all times and, crucially, present. Because once you've put in the hard work and prepared properly, you

 can afford to live in the moment. Great sportsmen and women have to be aware of what's happening around them – mentally and emotionally as well as spatially. The Swiss, despite their love of punctuality and time-keeping, are very good at being in the moment. 'They don't tend to rush off or feel they

have to be somewhere else,' says Diccon, 'they're happy to linger, to experience things.' Psychologists at Harvard University have found that the ability to remain present and live in the here and now can benefit our mental well-being and keep us happier. Advantage 'Federerism'.

When they're done smelling the roses/their fellow Swiss, they get active. 'There's a lot of skiing or hiking in the mountain air and most Swiss people feel a deep connection with nature,' says Stephan. Federer likes to do both, with aplomb, just FYI (thank you Google images...), often accompanied by his former tennis pro wife and their four children (FOUR!). Proximity to nature and exercising outdoors have both been proven to make us happier, so 'Federerism' dictates that we should all get a daily dose of both. Match point Roger/The Swiss.

Finally, 'Federerism' means consistency. It's no use being brilliant one day and about as much use as a soiled sweatband the next. The Swiss have been telling everyone they're 'quite all right thanks very much' for years now and report equal levels of happiness whether they take the 'Are you happy?' surveys in French, German or Italian. Clever old trilingual Swiss. The Swiss can be a conservative – some say 'narrow-minded' – bunch, where tradition is just as important as innovation. So while they have embraced some tenets of modern life (like Velcro...), they still keep Sundays sacrosanct with shops shut and an emphasis on spending time with family. They are faultlessly polite, reserved, and rich but not ostentatiously so. Federer is an ambassador for Rolex, but always selects their least bling watches and looks 'wealthy but not flashy', as my sound recordist puts it. When Swiss Open officials were searching for just the right gift for the multimillionaire sports star in 2003 to congratulate him on his achievements, they gave him a cow. Federer was so polite and thanked them so profusely, with such a good *A cow! Just what I always wanted!'* face, that they gave him another one a few years later.

Embracing 'Federerism' means good manners, discipline, mastery and controlling all variables so that there is very little that can go wrong. An approach to life that's aspirational yet achievable and eminently exportable – plus you don't have to care two hoots about sport. Game, set, match 'Federerism'.

HOW TO MAKE 'FEDERERISM' PART OF YOUR LIFE

1

Get really, really good at something...then don't show off about it.
Be courteous, always. And to everyone.

2

Prepare for every eventuality. You may not need to pack a
Swiss Army knife daily but you can get your affairs in order, plan ahead,
make your packed lunch, put something in the diary for the following
weekend, write down your career goals and work out what steps
are needed to get there.

3

Live in the moment – once you're properly prepared, you're free to play
the game with finesse and flair, without fear of things going wrong.

TARAB

Tarab, noun, musically induced ecstasy or enchantment. In use since medieval times to describe music and musicians, the term was popularised during the Ottoman Empire. Today *tarab* is used to describe the heightened emotional effect of certain types of music in Arab culture, especially in Syria. It is also associated with a traditional form of compositions featuring the oud, a lute-like stringed instrument.

SYRIA

Despite fertile plains, high mountains, red deserts and renowned 'road to...' moments of enlightenment en route to its capital, Syria is a place not normally associated with happiness. The country has endured numerous invasions and occupations over the ages, and then in 2011 a peaceful uprising against the president rapidly escalated into full-scale civil war. More than half of Syria's 21.1 million population have been displaced and the devastation continues. Madian, a friend of a friend, was forced to leave his home in Damascus in 2015 and became one of the 51,000 Syrians who made Austria their new home. He now lives in Vienna and tells me that although many of us have an impression of Syria from television or newspaper reports, there's another story, too.

'I miss my home, of course, but at least I have my life. Here, now – when many have lost theirs,' says Madian, '– so we have to keep going, to find a way to be happy again.' There's a sense that sustaining an apposite level of anguish for the situation is impossible – and so, he tells me, 'We get on with it. And there are still things that bring pleasure.' For Madian these include seeing friends, good food, horses (he's a keen equestrian and used to ride in Damascus), and *tarab*.

'We have a very strong cultural legacy in Syria,' Madian tells me, and although much of the country's heritage has been harmed by war (all six of the country's Unesco World Heritage sites have been damaged) many traditional art forms have been preserved in perpetuity. The internet not only allows Syrians to keep in touch with loved ones – wherever they have ended up in the world – it's also a connection to their culture. 'When the homeland of your youth is gone and you don't know when you'll see it again,' says Madian, '– it's good to be able to watch videos of Syrian things on YouTube, like *tarab* music.'

'*Tarab* is...' he searches for just the right word and by the time he finds it he's already lost in reverie: '...magical. When we listen to *tarab* music we feel like we're in another life – like we are drunk on the music.' He's smiling now. 'It's very, very special.' To experience *tarab*, he tells me, one must listen attentively and for some time. 'We're not talking about a song that finishes in five minutes,' Madian says, '– we're talking thirty or forty minute songs – maybe an hour. It's music that takes you on a journey.'

Tarab-inspiring music is often centred around matters of the heart ('I'd say 80 per cent are love songs, the rest are about religion') and these get very deep, very quickly. Madian talks me through some of the terms I can expect to find in a typical piece of *tarab* music, such as *tushakil asi* or 'may you plant my myrtle'. 'This is a plant commonly planted on graves in Syria,' he tells me, 'so the idea is that you want to die before your beloved so you don't have to live without them'. Ditto *tatalie e qabri*, 'may you stand on my grave'; *takafuni*, 'may you enshroud me'; and *tuqbirni*, 'may you bury me'. So far, so sunny. 'We do talk about death quite a lot when we talk about love,' Madian admits, 'but we don't really mean it...' He tells me that there's currently a running joke amongst Syrians: 'We say that after our crisis and the number of dead people that maybe God responded to us because we kept repeating these words, '*tuqbirni-takafuni-tushakil asi* etc.' Humour thrives in the direst of circumstances.

Tarab is quintessentially Arabic and relies on instruments not found elsewhere, like the oud, as well as unique arrangements like *maqamat*, which refers to a set of notes played in habitual patterns with a distinct melodic development. To experience *tarab* for myself, Madian prescribes me a series of YouTube gems. I watch Farid al-Atrash, the late Egyptian-

Syrian singer known as 'King of the Oud'. There's also Sabah Fakhri, an iconic tenor from Aleppo who interacts with his audience throughout – insisting that the auditorium lights remain on so that he can read the crowd. And finally, there's the late Umm Kulthum. Whatever you had planned after you'd finished reading this, cancel it. Set aside a good hour and listen to Umm Kulthum instead. The singer, known variously as 'Star of the Orient', 'The Voice of Egypt' and even 'Egypt's Fourth Pyramid', was lauded by Bob Dylan, Maria Callas and Bono (but don't let that put you off...). Her raw emotion won her adulation the world over and she's the most famous person I'd never heard of. In common with all *tarab* performances, time was of no fixed constraint to Kulthum and the duration of each song varied based on the level of interaction with her audience as well as her mood on the night. Live performances of one of her most popular songs, 'Ya Zalemni', ranged from forty-five to ninety minutes and she was apt to repeat a single line over and over, altering the emphasis each time until she brought audiences to the brink of euphoria – or *tarab*. 'Music like this just has an incredible power to move you and change the way you think about things,' says Madian, '– and yes, it makes you happier, too.'

Numerous studies have shown how music can alter our mood and I've long been a fan of a psychological tool called 'emotional arousal', whereby you watch a film or listen to music that makes you feel fired up and charged with energy. This can help you to tackle something daunting – from a scary meeting to making a tough decision. But music is also at the heart of culture – central to many of the major ceremonies of life as well as a backdrop to our leisure time. Music gives us an identity, uniting people, as well as helping to cross boundaries. A study published in the International Social Science Journal in 2016 found that in a world characterised by migration, music becomes an integral way for immigrants to negotiate and develop their identities in a new setting. For the displaced millions from Syria, music has never been more crucial. There's even a UNESCO-funded programme in Lebanon aiming to preserve the musical heritage of Syria and the region, offering classes in theory and the history of Arabic music and teaching students the oud.

I'm incredibly grateful to Madian for my introduction to Syrian music, and feel inspired to develop my knowledge of the region. But I can't help wondering whether any Western music might qualify as *tarab*-inducing. 'No,' he says, followed by: 'no, no, no, no, no.' *Say what you really feel, Madian...* 'But then, that's just me,' he adds as a qualifier: 'So maybe, yes.' It's a debate that simmers in the depths of specialist music chat-rooms, with classical music and even musical theatre scores mooted as possible contenders. A few brave souls even equate *tarab* with 'free form jazz', for which I apologise unreservedly to Madian and all Syrians everywhere. My own knowledge of classical music is woefully route one, but the crashing crescendo of Beethoven's *Ode to Joy* certainly has a similar effect on me to Madian's description of *tarab*. Or opera. Often described as an out-of-the-body experience, the basis of most opera is love and death – a lot like in *tarab* music. A 2012 study published in everyone's favourite beach read, *Transplantation Proceedings*, found that mice who were played Verdi's *La Traviata* during recovery from a heart transplant (don't ask...) lived almost four times longer than mice who were denied their fill of opera. So *tarab* is essentially life support. It seems likely that we in the West can enjoy the benefits of *tarab* music with the caveat that it should be something a little meatier than our average listening fare. It's near impossible to cover

the breadth of ecstasy and despair required for *tarab* in a three-minute pop song and the listener needs time to be taken on a 'journey'.

'Of course, there's nothing like listening to *tarab* music live,' Madian tells me just as I'm preparing to say goodbye. 'It's an amazing feeling when the audience gets really involved and it's the communal part I still miss. With live music it's like you aren't alone any more, for a while at least.' Researchers from Imperial College London found that seeing live music reduced levels of stress hormones and Patrick Fagan, an expert in behavioural science and associate lecturer at Goldsmith's University, found that those who attended a live concert saw their mood boosted by 21 per cent. Madian tells me how he used to go to performances all the time back home. 'It was completely normal,' he says, 'and when you live with something every day, you can take it for granted. But then it's gone. And you feel as though something in you has gone, too.'

This is a sentiment I dwell on for days.

There is much to be said for experiencing the emotional and imaginative truths of music as often as you can, as easily as you can – online or in the privacy of your own earphones. But making the most of the freedoms we have and listening to music live suddenly seems profoundly worthwhile. There is a direct connection when you're standing in front of another human being and listening to them. And doing so in the company of strangers – people you may not know yet but with whom you can share a transformative moment – is an experience like no other. 'Music should make you feel something,' Madian emails me the following week – be it greater sympathy, empathy, or even self-knowledge. So embrace the goose bumps. Say 'yes' to the next opportunity for live music. Seek out your own education in *tarab*-inducing music. Then, let the hairs on your arms settle and see how the world looks different afterwards.

HOW TO EXPERIENCE *TARAB*

1

Find some music that makes you feel something.
Really feel something. Apathy is not an option. We need to experience
being alive in all its incarnations, then remember our humanity
and charge ourselves for change.

2

Listen live if you can for extra goose bumps. Take friends or make new
ones with the people you're sharing the experience with.

3

Cry. Laugh. Feel. Get it all out. We're in this together.

4

Stuck or blocked? Take inspiration from Madian's listening suggestions.

5

Make the most of the life you have, right now.

MAI PEN RAI

One of the most commonly used phrases in Thailand, *mai pen rai* (pronounced *'my-pen-rye'*), is often translated as meaning 'never mind', 'don't worry', or 'it doesn't matter'. It is employed to minimise conflict and reduce tension wherever possible, but it's also a linchpin of Thai culture, a philosophy for living and a reminder of the importance of acceptance.

THAILAND

So you've had a bad day. You didn't get the promotion you were after; you had to skip lunch; experienced full-voltage hunger by 4 p.m., then got cut up in traffic on the way home. Sucks to be you, right? Or perhaps you just need a crash course in *mai pen rai*.

'People always think *mai pen rai* means we don't care: but it's not indifference,' says Pharinee, a colleague of a friend, from Bangkok. Rather than being a catchall phrase to lubricate social situations (though, also, *that...*) *mai pen rai* is about acceptance and a very Thai approach to life. 'If I hope to get something and I don't get it, I'll tell myself, *mai pen rai*, meaning "It's OK, it's not my time, I'll do something else instead,"' says Pharinee. 'You have to let it go. This is the Thai philosophy.'

Around 90 per cent of Thailand's 65-million-strong population identify as Buddhist – a religion that's big on letting go – but Thailand's history has given its people a distinctive slant on the idea of getting your Elsa on. For hundreds of years, Thailand operated under a patronage system whereby kings and landed gentry looked after the land and those who worked on it. But in 1932, amidst the rumblings of civil unrest, the country (then called Siam) transformed from an absolute monarchy to a constitutional monarchy. Thailand as a nation had to adopt a collective attitude of *mai pen rai* to sustain itself during this instability. King Bhumibol Adulyadej began his reign in 1946 pledging to 'reign with righteousness for the benefit and happiness of the Siamese people' – a promise he kept, by and large, becoming revered by all. But his reign also bore witness to eleven successful military coups and seven attempted coups – the last in 2014. When he died, in 2016, the whole country was plunged into mourning

for a year with yet more turbulence ensuing. Thai people, once again, had to draw on their *mai pen rai* to keep going.

As a largely agricultural country, with 40 per cent of the population involved in agribusiness, the *mai pen rai* approach has proved crucial. King Bhumibol Adulyadej was very active in promoting rural development during his reign, introducing more than 4,000 agricultural projects, from

irrigated reforestation to dairy farming. He also advocated self-sufficiency, encouraging farmers to grow enough food for their personal needs with a little left over to sell or barter. 'The King did a really good job selling us on agriculture and farming is a prized vocation in Thailand,' says Warinporn, a friend of a friend (Italy's Chiara, in fact) from just outside Bangkok. 'Farming is a respected and celebrated way of life in Thailand but it's also dependent on a lot of factors you can't do much about.' If a crop fails, there is nothing to be done but to accept it. *Mai pen rai.* Just as with Japanese *wabi-sabi*, the Thai philosophy is that nature is something to be accepted and celebrated rather than resisted. 'We grow up understanding that much of life – the weather, the heat, the harvest, etc. – is out of our control, so we may as well accept it when things happen, then move on.' The Stoics would be proud.

That's not to say that Thai people aren't trying to ensure that things turn out for the best. '*Mai pen rai* isn't about avoiding responsibility,' says Pharinee – this would be the antithesis of the teachings of Buddhism, where adherents are supposed to assume responsibility not only for their own lives but those of every living thing around them. Instead, *mai pen rai* is about what we can realistically do ourselves without inconveniencing others. 'It's essentially the sustainable mental manifesto,' says Warinporn. 'Being self-sufficient, having my own place, growing my own crops, that's happiness for me.' And *mai pen rai* is intricately linked with resilience and self-sufficiency, 'because the last thing you ever want to do is cause other people any trouble – this is a big part of our culture and how we were raised,' she says. There's even a habit of rejecting help or an offer simply because Thais don't want to cause trouble or inconvenience to another person.

Self-sufficiency and acceptance of your lot in life bleeds into other terms used frequently in Thailand. There's *por dee*, or 'it fits'. 'You don't have to be rich but you can have *por dee* money to sustain you,' says Warinporn – a lot like with Swedish *lagom*. Likewise a dress can be *por dee* with your body and you can have a job that's *por dee* with your lifestyle. There's also *sabai* – to be comfortable or in good health – often used in duplicate to mean 'calm down'. 'You hear *sabai sabai* a lot in Thailand,' says Pharinee, 'especially when you want to tell someone not to take life too seriously, or to just enjoy themselves.' And then there's *jai yen*, or 'cool heart'. 'This is another way to tell someone to calm down,' says Warinporn. 'My husband says that to me a lot.' Apparently she doesn't mind, either. *Mai pen rai...*

'Staying calm, not losing your cool and accepting what we can't change frees Thais from many of the petty upsets and irritations that plague modern life,' says Warinporn. 'We just keep smiling through it.' Thailand is known as the 'Land of Smiles' in tourist brochure-speak and smiling is such an art form that there are different genres of grinning in Thailand. A few of my favourites include:

Yim cheun chom – the 'I admire you' smile

Yim thak thaan – the 'I disagree, but still, carry on with your crazy idea...' smile

Yim sao – the sad smile

Yim mai awk – the 'I'm trying to smile but I can't quite manage it and my eyes are hating you right now' smile

'We don't always smile because we're happy,' says Warinporn. 'We're not fools: and we're not always happy. We just smile on the *outside*.' Ouch. 'Thai people are good in the service industry,' she tells me. 'They know how to serve and that they should smile to earn money – and it works.' But faking it can also be beneficial for happiness, since tricking our brain into believing we're happy releases feel-good hormones including dopamine and serotonin. Researchers at the University of Kansas found that a forced smile helps reduce stress, lowers our heart rate and helps body and mind recover more quickly after a taxing task. So smiling keeps you *jai yen*, too. 'People aren't very aggressive or assertive in Thailand – it's not in our culture,' says Warinporn. 'So we'd much rather smile than fall out with you. We're not fans of confrontation or pushing ourselves – or other people – too hard.'

The late King Bhumibol Adulyadej, a man not prone to extremes, championed all forms of religion practised in the kingdom, acknowledging and advocating the importance of diversity. He endorsed 'walking the middle ground' as the route to happiness and counselled his people that 'as long as you don't put in too much extra effort or go beyond your capabilities, you'll be content,' Pharinee tells me, before clarifying: 'It's not that you can't want to do a good job, it's just that you should want what's within your manageable range.' Instead of striving all the time for more, *mai pen rai* means that the way you live your life now is good for you – you shouldn't worry or want too much more. A simple, eminently sensible approach that has helped make Thais happier. It's not about acquiring riches or becoming rictus-grin-musical-theatre-star-on-ketamine happy: it's about having enough, being enough (again, see *'lagom'*) and accepting when things don't go your way – something Thais are well practised at. Thailand has been ranked as the least miserable country out of sixty-six economies for a fourth consecutive year, according to Bloomberg's 'Misery Index' for 2018. A suitably understated *jai yen* accolade.

Thais don't know what the future holds. Since King Bhumibol Adulyadej passed away, many now feel that the country's problems have been magnified, with political unrest, pollution and traffic problems at their worst for years. 'The King was also very good at bringing people together,' says Warinporn, 'and we miss that. But I think the Thai mentality will persist. We'll always have *mai pen rai.*'

What she said.

HOW TO ADOPT A *MAI PEN RAI* APPROACH TO LIFE

1

Put things in context. So your wifi is down? You'll survive. *Mai pen rai.*
Traffic terrible? You'll get there eventually. Or you won't. *Mai pen rai.*
Flight delayed? Stop and think about the fact that we can
actually put people in a big metal tube that can fly through the air
like a bird: that's amazing. *Mai pen rai.*

2

Consider your harvest – be it crops, campaigns or coursework: do all you
can and then accept that you can do no more. *Mai pen rai.*

3

Feeling frustrated? Try three deep breaths, just like your mother used
to say, and up your 'cool heart' credentials.

4

Smile – turning that frown upside down makes you happier and
healthier, even if you're faking it.

5

Be more sustainable: can you keep up the seventy-hour working week,
burning the candle at both ends? Without a stomach ulcer? Probably
not. Find your middle path and stick to it.

GEZELLIG

Gezellig (pronounced *'heh-sell-ick'*), adjective, from Middle Dutch *gesellich* or 'companionable', now used to mean cosy or quaint. Can also be used as a noun, *gezelligheid*, to refer to a positive, warm emotion or a feeling of togetherness. Employed liberally in everyday conversation in The Netherlands where all things *gezellig* are cherished. Similar to Danish *hygge* or German *Gemütlichkeit* in some respects, but *gezellig* also has an emphasis on the old. Plus the Dutch think that they came up with the concept first...

THE
NETHERLANDS

'Coffee and cake is *gezellig*; going for a beer is *gezellig*; watching TV can be *gezellig* – especially if you have *gezellige* friends over. A room can be *gezellig*; a building can be *gezellig*; a person can be *gezellig*; a whole evening can be *gezellig*,' my friend Wouter from The Hague begins my schooling. So can anything be *gezellig*? 'Pretty much,' he tells me: 'although old stuff tends to be extra *gezellig*.' Unlike in Denmark where Scandi modern chic can still qualify as *hygge*, going Dutch means going old. So traditional shops and boutiques are *gezellig*; modern interiors and warehouses are not. The *bruine kroegen* or old-fashioned 'brown cafes' with dark wood interiors and low lighting that litter Amsterdam are the epitome of *gezellig* – as are local *kroeg* bars ('old man pubs' for British readers), which can function as an extension of one's own living room. 'Basically, if it's nice and cosy, it's *gezellig*,' clarifies Wouter, '– and we use *gezellig* All The Time. Even more than the Danes use *hygge*.' I tell him this is quite the claim, and he says: 'It's true! We didn't think there was another word like *gezellig* in the world – we actually thought we had invented the concept of cosy nice times, so were kind of mad when *hygge* became this worldwide thing coming out of Denmark,' he says, before clarifying: 'Well, not "mad", but, you know, "surprised"...' and I nod. Because I haven't seen Wouter mad in the five years I've known him, and because the Dutch are distinctly laid-back.

Along with *gezellig* , liberalism and tolerance are key to Dutch happiness. 'We've been squeezed by so many other countries over the years, we've had to learn to get along,' explains Wouter. The Netherlands is made up of twelve provinces, and borders Germany to the east and Belgium to the south. Famously flat, 'Netherlands' literally means 'lower countries' and only 50 per cent of its land is more than a metre above sea level. The Dutch have a strange, love-hate relationship with the water that's constantly threatening to engulf the land. With a population of 17 million, they have one of the highest population densities in the world (414 people per square kilometre) – and there's no choice but for everyone to compromise and co-operate. A notably secular country, The Netherlands regards religion as a personal matter up to the individual - and the Dutch have a long history of social tolerance. Abortion, prostitution and euthanasia are all legal, and The Netherlands was the world's first country to legalise same-sex marriage in 2001. The country also ranks second highest in the world's Press Freedom Index and has a famously progressive drugs policy.

'We're a trading nation,' says Wouter – in fact, The Netherlands is the world's second-largest exporter of food and agricultural products after the US – 'and we have so many nationalities that we've had to be pretty open to new ideas and different ways of living.' My friend Cindy, also from The Hague, tells me: 'We don't have many traditions in The Netherlands, so we feel free to pick the best of the cultures we have around us.' Wouter

agrees. Growing up, his family would have Chinese food for Christmas every year, because they liked it best and because the well-established Chinese community where he lived meant that the ingredients were readily available along with the expertise to make the dishes authentically. The Netherlands' small but significant Turkish population shares its own country's traditions and there's a strong Moroccan influence in some regions. There is an openness to most Dutch people that is refreshing to outsiders. I first visited in 1999 when my friend Tony and I hitch-hiked to Amsterdam, something that in retrospect appears alarmingly ill advised but at the time seemed a perfectly sane way to spend a weekend. We were struck by the unexpectedly picturesque views experienced from out of the windows of some pretty huge lorries (and, latterly, a Lada) as well as by just how nice all the Dutch folk we met were. Was there something in the water?

Could *gezellig*, windmills and weed really make the Dutch so seemingly sorted?

'We have our moments!' Cindy assures me, 'but we are pretty open to being friendly and chatting to anyone really. It's *gezellig*, and we are *gezellig*-curious about the world around us and the people we meet – so we're not afraid to open our mouth and be direct.' In contrast to the *hygge* Danes, who can be reserved with new people, and the Germans, who keep their *Gemütlichkeit* private, it's as though the Dutch have enough *gezellig* to go around for everyone. The Netherlands is

consistently ranked one of the happiest countries in the world and the Dutch have one of the shortest working weeks, clocking in an average of just 30.4 hours according to OECD data.

'Many people work part time, especially parents,' says Cindy, 'because childcare is still expensive.' In The Netherlands, mothers are expected back at work when babies are around ten weeks old – but only part-time – and dads, grandparents and extended family often share out the week between them. Still, going back to work ten weeks post-birth doesn't sound very *gezellig*. Cindy admits that it's not, but tells me that the Dutch do have something else going for them here: a sort of *gezellig*-enforcer. Benefits to new mothers include access to a live-in maternity nurse, or 'doula', covered by insurance, who will come to your home for a few days to care for parents as well as taking on 'cooking, light cleaning and childcare' duties. Wouter still gets emotional recalling the doula who helped out when his son was born. 'She was WONDERFUL!' He presses both palms down on the table to emphasise his point before telling me that she would send him down for a nap when he looked tired. *You as in 'the dad'?!* I ask, incredulous. He nods wistfully: 'Sometimes she'd even suggest I have a beer, too. It was very, very *gezellig*.' I'll bet... Once new parents are back at work, there's a pretty sensible *gezellig* approach to paid labour whereby you get your work done, then go home – presenteeism be damned. If you're sick in The Netherlands, you stay at home for some *uitzieken* – literally 'outsicking' to 'sick it out', letting the illness run its course rather than staggering in to infect your workmates. Lemsip and duvet days all around.

For anyone not yet won around to the *gezellig* delights of The Netherlands, they also have tulips, clogs, an obsession with Miffy (Dick Bruna, RIP) and bikes. Everywhere. Thirty-six per cent of Dutch people cite cycling as their 'most frequent mode of transport' according to European Commission data and it keeps them healthy and happy. They also eat wholesome, 'farmer-food' as my friend puts it – indulging their sweet tooth regularly as anyone who's ever visited a *gezellig bruine kroegen* and sampled *stroopwafel* ('syrup waffle') can testify, but also going heavy on the meat and two veg with a side of dairy. And the Dutch love their milk. During my first trip to a Dutch workplace, I was tickled to see suited businessmen and women downing cartons of milk – but this isn't unusual. Many will neck the white stuff to wash down the national lunch dish of a simple cheese sandwich. Milk is a source of calcium and vitamin D, both important for regulating mood, while cheese contains a chemical called casein, which can trigger the brain's opioid receptors, producing a feeling of euphoria, according to researchers from the University of Michigan. And – pub quiz fact alert – all this protein helps to make them the tallest people in the world (honestly – there's a Dutch boy in my son's class who I swore was the teacher when he started...). 'We tend to eat well

and we know how to live well, too,' says Cindy, adding, 'I'd say most Dutchies have a glass of wine most nights. Or two. Maybe three.' *Three?* She nods: 'That's pretty normal. But we don't binge drink.' *Right. No...*

The morning after the night before, there's always coffee to get you going again. A Harvard study from 2011 found that drinking coffee lowered the rate of depression among women, while a 2012 study from Ruhr University, Germany, found that caffeine stimulates parts of the brain connected to positivity. According to a Euromonitor study the Dutch drink the most coffee in the world – and they're still one of the most laid-back nations on earth. One can only imagine that without a caffeine hit, they would be positively horizontal. Frank Sinatra once described orange as 'the happiest colour' – and since the Dutch dress in the acid tone that's the colour of their Royal Family at every available opportunity, it should be little surprise that they are very happy indeed.

In addition to *gezellig*, the happy Dutch have several other delectable words that I fully intend on adopting into my everyday lexicon, from the sensual *lekker*, adjective, meaning 'tasty' or 'sexy' (so Dutch...), to the delightful *feestvarken*, translated as 'party pig'. 'The party pig is someone in whose honour a party is being thrown,' Wouter tells me (FYI this sounds even more fun in a Dutch accent). And then there's the wonderfully invigorating *uitwaaien*

or 'walking in the wind for fun'. 'There's nothing like a *uitwaaien* on the beach,' says Wouter. 'The fresh air is so good for you and it always makes you feel better. We try to get to the water a lot and we'll go out of our way to get to nature as often as we can.' This is challenging in a country as crammed as The Netherlands. 'Traffic can be crazy,' Wouter says, 'but we will happily drive for an hour and three-quarters to get to the beach, then spend an hour trying to park – it's worth it.' And then when they come home again, windswept and weary, they can hunker down with some cheese (probably), get the wine out, and really get *gezellig*. I'm sold.

HOW TO GO DUTCH AND GET
GEZELLIGHEID

1

Find your *bruine kroegen* – or brown café – equivalent: an old local
where you feel right at home and are guaranteed a *gezellig* time.

2

Try being more friendly and open, Dutch-style, to everyone you meet.

3

Live well – and let live. Enjoy life and be the party pig
when occasion commands.

4

Run in the wind, whenever possible. There's something wonderfully
childlike and chaotic about the sensation of being blown about by
nature – and you'll never regret an *uitwaaien*.

5

If wine, windmills and weed don't make you happy, there's always clogs,
Miffy or bicycling. And if none of the above cut it for you, it's time
for a long hard look in the mirror...

KEYIF

Keyif (pronounced *'kay-if'*), noun, originally an Arabic term signifying 'mood, contentment, intoxication'. Variations on *keyif* can be found in Russian, Hebrew, Kurdish, Urdu and Hindi, but the term has become an institution in Turkey. Now taken to mean an enjoyable state of relaxation, the pursuit of idle pleasure is a national pastime and the definition of happiness for many Turks.

TURKEY

 The backgammon set is spread out in front of you, set up for a game that started hours ago but there's no hurry to finish it any time soon. The sun is setting after another hot, humid day and finally the air is cooling. You're with friends, sitting outside at a bar, looking out onto the glistening Bosporus – seemingly idle, but in fact enjoying the essential Turkish custom of *keyif*. Melis, a colleague originally from Istanbul, is painting me a vivid picture of her homeland during an uncharacteristically scorching day on a rooftop in central London. We are sticky and hot but there is no respite, no sea breeze, and we're both embroiled in an afternoon of meetings with no hope of a break anytime soon. And suddenly we both wish we could be teleported from the River Thames to the Turkish Straits.

Keyif is an integral part of day-to-day life in Turkey, with Istanbul its undisputed cultural capital. Melis describes her countryfolk's national pastime as 'a low-key passion for languor', because *keyif* is all about taking it slow. 'Relaxing is really important to Turks,' agrees Olivia, also from Istanbul, and to truly get *keyif* you need to take it easy. 'There's no need to get complicated with *keyif*,' she says. 'It should be about celebrating the simple pleasures in life – like swimming, or walking on the beach or watching a sunset. Everyone does it – it's not a class thing and it doesn't discriminate – *keyif* is inclusive.' It's also a salve in troubled times. 'You may not be happy in life generally,' says Olivia, 'but with *keyif* you can decide that here, in this moment, you're going to enjoy yourself. And we need this right now.'

Turkey ranks below average in income, wealth, health, education and earnings according to OECD data – with only 51 per cent of 15- to 64-year-olds having a paid job. The country straddles the continents of Europe and Asia, bordered by Greece, Bulgaria, Georgia, Armenia, Azerbaijan, Iran, Iraq and Syria, and Turkey's 80 million strong population have endured decades of civil war and an attempted coup in 2016. 'The situation here has always been volatile – it's always fluctuated, and things can literally change from one month to the next,' says Olivia of her homeland. 'We tend not to make commitments to do things in future because we don't know what will happen in two weeks' time, so we take each day as it comes.' *Bakarız, inşallah* – or 'We'll see, God willing' – is a phrase heard often when making plans. So if someone says 'I'd like to have you over for coffee some time soon' you might respond, *Bakarız, inşallah!* 'But the one thing Turks have in all this unsettlement is the idea of *keyif*,' says Olivia, '– and *keyif* keeps us together.' It's telling that the sole metric at which Turkey excels in the happiness surveys is 'civic participation', and 86 per cent of Turks believe that they know someone they could rely on in times of need, according to the OECD. Although many Turks can't 'fix' what's happening around them, they can always rely on friends, family and *keyif*.

The term is so pervasive in Turkish culture that it can be attached to a variety of 'activities' – or, as is often the case, 'non-activities' – when *keyif* becomes *keyfi*. So watching TV can be elevated into *televizyon keyfi* so long as you're slobbing on the sofa in something elasticated and feeling consciously present and free from stress. You can add *keyif* or *keyfi* to the end of anything you want to do such as *kitap okuma keyfi* or 'book reading *keyif*'; *bira keyfi* or 'beer *keyif*'; and even Pazar *keyfi* or 'Sunday *keyif*'.

'Because *keyif* is about doing things in a relaxed way, you can use it for most things,' explains Melis. There's *gezme keyfi* or 'strolling *keyif*', where you arrange to meet someone and then just walk and talk aimlessly ('I can recommend!' says Melis). Then there's *meyhane keyfi* – drinking rakı and eating meze at a restaurant. Rakı (without a dot over the i) is produced by twice distilling grape pomace (the solid, leftover munge) then flavouring it with aniseed. Turkey's national drink is served with a side of water that you pour into your rakı until it turns a cloudy white colour. 'We call it "Lion's Milk",' Melis tells me, presumably because it looks fairly innocent but is, as my guide tells me, 'really, really strong'. Taking tentative swigs of your Lion's Milk and picking at your food is an 'activity' that can last for hours, with friends or family sitting around a big table, chatting and eating with no concern for the time. 'It's not like in London where they want your table back in two hours,' says Melis. 'In Turkey, we might start at 8 p.m. then go on until one or two in the morning.' Another important term for Turks is *çakırkeyif*, meaning 'tipsy *keyif*', Olivia tells me. 'This just means that you're not drunk and you're not totally sober, but you've got your buzz on.' *Çakırkeyif* = #weekendgoals

There's also *mangal keyfi* – barbecuing, where you create a DIY restaurant-by-the-Bosporus or any open-air greenery and grill vegetables, chicken, fish, or lamb chops. You'll see big groups of people with their tongs, their music, their cool-boxes of food and a huge flask of tea. Tea is important in Turkish culture and so naturally, there's *çay keyfi* or 'tea *keyif*' – going round to friends' or neighbours' for tea, cake and a good gossip. Turkish tea is made from loose leaves (no bags, please) and served black in petite curvy tea glasses. Coffee is big, too, and there may even be

someone reading your *fal*, or 'fortune'. 'You drink your very strong, thick, mud-like coffee then turn the grounds out onto a saucer and wait for the sediment to settle to predict your future,' Melis tells me. Younger people are into it too – mostly females and mostly just for fun – but the dedicated can take a trip to town to see some of the elderly women who read coffee fortunes for a living. 'They can be surprisingly accurate,' Melis assures me as I try to mask my scepticism. 'Honestly! I don't believe in it but it's still freaky how true some of them are.' I promise to try, on the proviso that I can sample some *çakırkeyif* afterwards.

If you've still got some energy left after all this relaxing, there's nothing Turks like more than indulging in *Boğaz keyfi*, with a stroll along the Bosporus. This is such an iconic part of Turkish culture that songs and poems are written about it and every Turkish film has at least one scene of a Bosporus stroll. Looking out to sea and marvelling at the glittering Bosporus, you can also lay claim to the greatest *keyif* ever, Istanbul *keyfi*. 'People from Istanbul can relax like no one else,' says Melis, though she admits she may not be impartial: 'we're really good at *keyif*.'

Keyif is so hallowed that there are a lot of phrases associated with making sure someone's pleasure and enjoyment isn't compromised in Turkey, like '*Keyifin yerinde mi?*' ('Are you feeling OK?'). There's also

'*Keyifini çıkar!*' – a common phrase used to mean 'Enjoy it!' And the ultimate compliment used to describe 'someone who prioritises pleasure': '*keyfine düşkün bir insan*'. But this level of *keyif* isn't anything we can actively pursue. 'If you're trying too hard, that's just not *keyif*,' Olivia tells me, as I struggle not to appear crestfallen. 'The moment you start putting a lot of effort into something, it stops being *keyif*,' she says. So if a host gets too serious about the décor or the food or whatever it is you're doing/not-doing, you can miss the *keyif*. 'This is because *keyif* isn't about the way things look,' says Olivia: 'It's about comfort and ease. You have to just...chill.'

Chilling is cherished in Turkey and 'taking it easy' is held in high esteem. 'So if someone's working on a job, we'll say *kolay gelsin*, which means "may it be easy for you",' Melis explains. 'We say it all the time – you might say it to someone in the office in the morning, or you could pass some construction workers on the street and you'll say it to them.' Turks even say '*kolay gelsin*' to people at the gym (now that's my kind of workout...). For Turks, relaxing your body and mind *keyif*-style is an art form – not something to be derided and never something to be rushed.

'Maybe it's the heat, or maybe it's everything we've had to deal with historically, but *keyif* really is treasured in Turkey,' says Melis. She tells me that this essence of Turkey is something that can be hard to export to the rest of the world. 'But I keep trying,' she adds. And now you can, too.

HOW TO EXPERIENCE *KEYIF*

1

Take a break from the hustle. You may not have the Bosporus, but I'll bet
there's a pond nearby. Or a lake. Or a river.

2

Eat at a more leisurely pace.
See how long you can stretch dinner out for.
Play backgammon (already a regular? Well done you.
Bonus *keyif* points!).

3

Do more staring into the middle distance or as far as you can see and
observe how you feel afterwards. Remember to b.r.e.a.t.h.e.

4

Enjoy idleness, guilt-free. *Kolay gelsin!*

HOMEYNESS

Homeyness, noun, possessing the quality of being homey. First used in the mid 19th century to confer the comforting attributes of something being 'like home'. Used to describe a cosy, intimate quality, often applied to interiors or hand-crafted items and typically implying something unpretentious and unsophisticated. A throwback to simpler times.

USA

Nora sits at the table she grew up with – the one bought for $18 from a now defunct textile mill in her once-boomtown hometown – and studies the lacy patina made up of all the tiny scratch marks made by a hundred years of scissors and needles. She imagines the rows of women who made the marks – women like her, trying to make something a bit better for their families. 'I've sometimes lived like those long-ago seamstresses did,' Nora tells me. 'I've bathed my children in tubs in the living room when the hot water went out, sloshing the soapy water off the front porch when they're done. I've prepared holiday meals on two square feet of counter space, and I've felt a connection – a sort of camaraderie – with everyone who was in this place before me, working with their hands here.' Nora sews, bakes, crochets and derives a particular satisfaction from painting decorative wooden letters for her children and the children of friends. 'I think of them the whole time I'm making them, at the table, lost in a tiny, happy world.' Sometimes she takes breaks from letter painting to sew a doll or mix up something 'to make the house smell delicious and that can be slathered with butter'. For Nora, this is soothing: 'My head and my hands hum together and everything imperfect feels perfectly fine for a little while.'

This is 'homeyness'. Not to be confused with 'homeliness', meaning dowdy or plain and unattractive, or 'homie', slang for homeboy/homegirl. 'Homeyness' – or the quality of being homey – conjures up images of cushions, collections, crocheting, craft tables and A Lot of wood. Basically, it's the mood board for Winona Ryder's 1995 film *How to Make an American Quilt*. And it's BIG in America. Steph, a friend of a friend from Massachusetts, tells me that for somewhere to feel 'homey', it has to be comfortable and welcoming. 'It's the smell of my mom's chicken soup and baking bread,' she says. 'It should be clean enough that I don't feel anxious about things that need to be done, but have enough decoration or clutter to feel lived-in'. Anything too modern feels cold – and cool is the antithesis of 'homeyness'.

Drew, a knitter from Salt Lake City, tells me that 'homey' is about warmth and closeness: 'It's sharing, together in a happy atmosphere,' he tells me. 'So yes, I like a home that is aesthetically pleasing, but it's more about fostering special moments than having a place that looks nice.' 'Homeyness' is prioritising comfort over style – which means the pared-back, functional minimalism of Scandinavia can come as something of a shock to Americans. The mother of my friend Jason from Boston was so taken aback when she first visited his all-white Scandi-pad in Denmark ('Jason! It's like a SPACESHIP!') that she asked if she needed to 'speak into a panel to open the bathroom door' ('Er…no…?'). 'Homeyness' isn't about fast-paced urban living, either – instead, it's an excuse to slow things down. Rachel, a quilter, knitter and embroidery fan from California says: '"Homey" means embracing the mundane of life. There's something about crafting that forces you to slow down.' It's also a refuge from the big, bad world and a respite from modern life. Ostrich syndrome isn't tenable long-term – nor is it desirable. But as a ploy to regroup, restore energy and renew our compassion levels before heading back out into the fray, is there something to be said for 'homeyness'?

Nora thinks so. Post-financial crisis and Trump inauguration, The American Dream is under threat for many, and, as Nora says, 'Life hasn't turned out as we had planned.' The idea of a steady job that pays the bills and buys you a house with a white picket fence and enough left over to start a college fund for your 2.4 children now seems the stuff of fantasy. When Nora and her husband had their first baby, they were still renting an apartment but longed to give their son the childhood they remembered.

'I wanted a place that felt like home – even if it wasn't permanent,' Nora explains, 'so in the long tradition of determined mothers in less-than-ideal situations, I compensated like my life depended on it and began a serious relationship with all things crafting.'

More and more Americans are getting in on the act with half of US households taking part in at least one crafting activity, according to the Association For Creative Industries (AFCI). Nostalgia is a major motivation and Rachael, a cross-stitch fan from Florida who makes her own bread and soap, says: 'I love that I can do something that my grandmother and her elders did. We're consciously reconnecting with "older times".' Steph from Massachusetts adds: 'I love the idea of something being valued over generations. To own and use a blanket that was hand-crocheted by my great aunt is just awesome to me.'

All the crafters I speak to 'fess up to having a *Little House on the Prairie* alter ego and connection with the past in a 'new' country is often prized. In reality there's nothing 'new' about America. The first settlers came from Asia between 42,000 and 17,000 years ago, before old Christopher Columbus arrived in 1492, bringing with him the delights of European colonisers and a whole host of diseases that devastated the indigenous peoples. But the US celebrated the Declaration of Independence on 4 July 1776, when the Thirteen Colonies of America declared themselves to be states, no longer part of the British Empire, and for many this is when the country as we know it was born. Americans in Europe often observe

that everything is 'old' – from the customs to the architecture. In lieu of a similar legacy, many Americans develop a fascination with genealogy, with every American I've ever met telling me, in detail, about how they are 'one quarter this...' and 'an eighth that...'. The rise of DNA testing services such as 23andMe as well as 'pedigree mapping' via ancestry.com can be baffling to outside observers but *Time* magazine even ran an article calling genealogy 'the new porn' in America. As a nation of immigrants who have assimilated to some degree or another, there's a sense that by nailing down your past, you can feel less alone heading into your future.

The quilt can even be viewed as a metaphor for America itself and the different nationalities and cultures that make up the 'United' States. Just as a quilt is made up of many patches, each with its own colour, fabric and past, which are tacked, then stitched together to become something unified, America - at its best - is a collaboration and combination of its parts. In this respect, the quilt is a symbol of modern America - and one that seems preferable to the out of date 'melting pot' analogy or even the 'salad bowl' (because, as we all know, leaves wilt). The bedspread just got political. 'We're proud of being a country of immigrants but we also want to know where we're from,' as one friend puts it, '- we want our history'. 'Homeyness' has always been a major part of this and Hollywood set designers even seek out quilts, or knitted items to suggest a sense of past and family history for characters. Nosing around homes in the US over the years, I've often had the feeling that many Americans are dressing their 'set' in the same way - using 'homey' props and scenery to create a collage of their past and tell a story about their family and their values. And for those who have grown up in a digital world, the lure of connecting with the past and getting their homey on is stronger still.

The biggest crafters in the US today are younger than the average American, according to the AFCI, and millennials cite social media sources as an inspiration (just type *#crafting* into your preferred outlet and you too might catch the bug). But many also mention the appeal of doing something with their hands. 'Everything seems to be getting more automated, so making something tangible, with no screens to look at, feels grounding,' is how Rachael (the one with two 'a's who makes the soap. Keep up...), a self-confessed millennial, describes this impulse. There's also an environmental imperative. The trend for upcycling and *homey* crafting that reuses and treasures the 'old' is less wasteful than buying new each time. 'Millennials are very aware of our environment,' says Rachael. 'We're seeing the effects of what generations before have done – the Great Barrier Reef, entering another mass extinction in our oceans thanks to all our trash and plastic floating around, and we don't want that.' As well as saving the planet, 'homeyness' can save money – and this is important at a time when the economy and housing markets are in such dire straits. 'We have to make sure we're planning for retirement, since there's no guarantee of social security, or pensions, or help from employers anymore,' Rachael tells me. And there's something fundamental about making rather than buying for Americans. In a country wedded to the free market economy where everything seems to be for sale, 'homeyness' demonstrably isn't (or, at least, it shouldn't be.) As Steph says: '"Homeyness" for me is simply giving. It's a sense of comfort and love.'

At its essence, 'homeyness' isn't just raiding your local craft emporium for supplies then holing up to hide from the rest of the world; it is about togetherness and giving love. Knitting was promoted as a patriotic duty during the First World War and Americans were asked to knit 1.5 million garments for soldiers to keep them warm and offer them some comfort far from home in dangerous conditions. It became so popular that in 1915 the New York Philharmonic had to beg audience members to take a break from it as the clacking of needles was disrupting performances. In 1987 a group of strangers gathered in San Francisco to start the AIDS Memorial

Quilt, documenting the lives of those who they feared history might otherwise forget. Many still craft as part of a community for a good cause. Drew knits hats and scarves to donate to a local homeless shelter. 'This isn't totally selfless,' he tells me. 'I'm fortunate in that my hobby aligns well with the needs of others, and I like having a project to work on – but the Salt Lake City winters can be bitterly cold so it's good to do my bit.' Nora, Steph, Rachel and Rachael all mention that the joy their creations brings others is a major motivation and that keeping their passion as a hobby, rather than selling their wares, is a way of holding on to this special, simple purity.

More men are getting in on the 'homey' act, too, and although Drew is sometimes the only man at his 'knit circle', many of his male friends have also begun to knit or crochet as well. This is smart, since research from Harvard Medical School found that knitting reduces stress and can even lower blood pressure. Rachael learned about soap making from a male co-worker and knows another male crafter who's into floral arrangements. But, she notes, 'most men I know are – at least outwardly – into more traditionally "manly" activities like building and fixing things'. Rachael's husband has started learning basic woodworking skills. Nora's has become 'obsessed' with brewing beer – and studies show that more men are keen 'makers' than had been previously thought. Research from the remarkably un-'homey' sounding AFCI found that male participation in creative activities has been underreported in the past, with painting, drawing, wood crafts and home décor the modern gentlemen's favourites. One need only amble around Brooklyn today to see tribes of bearded hipsters on their single speed bikes furiously pedalling home to whittle something, knock out a watercolour, or work on their etchings.

Whatever you do *homey*-hobby wise, it's a plus in the happiness stakes. Science shows that challenging ourselves

 to do something different creates new neural pathways in the brain and learning a new skill can even make us happier, according to researchers from San Francisco State University. A British study published in the *Oxford Review of Education* found that participation in hobbies had a positive effect on well-being and the capacity to cope with stress. Learning a new skill also has an immediate impact on self-esteem and gives us a sense of purpose, according to University of London research, and helps broaden our social circle. Or, as my friend Becca from Texas beautifully phrases it, 'Quilting is community'.

Rachael agrees: 'It's hugely social – my mom will go to quilt groups where all these older ladies get together once a month, and while they're working on hand quilting, or piecing together quilt squares, they reminisce together and share stories. I love that personal connection.' Californian Rachel (the quilter) points out: 'If you think about American history – women have always gathered to create. Be it uniforms for officers or as an act of protest. So, the "homeyness" is how ladies bond.' It's also a way to show love.

Becca has fond memories of sleeping under heavy quilts and 'the feeling of love under those patches and stitches', and, as Steph says, 'if anyone spends a dozen hours or more hand-creating a gift like a blanket for you, it's because they love you.' 'I enjoy looking around and feeling the love we put into these projects,' agrees Rachael. Because creating something *homey* is a physical manifestation of love. And 'homeyness' represents happiness – or the closest thing many people can get to it right now in the US. So go forth and craft. Make your space 'homey' and your hobbies 'homier'. Then share them with others. And see how it feels.

HOW TO GET 'HOMEY'

1

Make something – be it biscuits, doilies, quilts, knitted wares, art or home-brewed beer; just do something with your hands.

2

Find your people, your community of old souls, and get together as often as you can to craft your 'homey' wares.

3

Share your creations and pay it forward with a gift that you've really thought about for someone you love.

4

Treasure gifts that someone has made for you. Appreciate the care and attention that has gone into it and know how much you mean to them.

5

Surrender to the clutter. Set aside your Scandi-design principles for a nano-second [note to self] and see how the claustrophobic love-hug of 'homeyness' feels for you. If it works, reconsider the chrome and make your house a 'homey' haven instead.

HWYL

Hwyl (pronounced *'h-oil'*), noun, a strong, stirring feeling of emotion, enthusiasm and fervour – integral to the national character. From the Welsh for the sail of a ship in full wind (*hwylio* is to go sailing), *hwyl* has come to mean giving something some welly or doing it with gusto. Also used to mean 'fun', 'goodbye', 'good luck' or 'all the best' (*'pob hwyl!'*).

WALES

A very nice boy from Porthcawl is marrying my mate Susie. I am sitting in a pew, listening to the vows, already in tears (this is standard...) and then the male voice choir starts up. And suddenly I'm heaving with snot-filled sobs, moved beyond all reason, and pretty sure I'm about to have a heart attack, so flooded do my insides feel. I'm not alone: our friend Becky's in bits and even my other half professes to having 'something in his eye'. Heading to Wales anytime soon? Pack hankies.

'We experience *hwyl* everywhere – from the rugby stands to singsongs down the pub, ministers in pulpits, and of course male voice choirs,' my friend Ben from Blaenafon tells me, explaining that this cornerstone of Welsh culture is positively sodden with *hwyl*. Music is central and even inanimate instruments can have *hywl* – particularly the brass section or a trombone. 'We like things big,' Ben tells me. 'I think Welsh people tend to be more open to big emotions than our Anglo-Saxon neighbours – and we're happy to talk about how we're feeling.' If a Welshman or woman is having a great day, you'll know about it – and vice versa. 'We don't do "bottling things up" and in Wales, everything's either the "best in the world" or the "worst in the world",' says Ben. 'We take pleasure in extremes – we can be very up and down'. He speaks in a lilting, singsong cadence that matches

his sentiment and because Ben and I have been friends for twenty years, I call him out on his vocal rollercoaster. 'That's because Wales is very up and down,' is his reply. 'I'm merely a product of my surroundings...' Ben is a successful actor and master of dialects, so he knows of whence he speaks. He explains how intonations tend to match the landscape in the best and most efficient way to make the voice carry. 'In the Fenlands, for example, it's very flat, and so the vowels

can be, too,' he says, '– but in the Welsh valleys, it's the opposite.' Just as the landscape and the inflection is comprised of peaks and troughs, so *hwyl* is a hotbed of fevered highs and dramatic lows.

'*Hwyl* isn't a cosy, warm thing: it's expansive and melancholic,' says Diane, the Welsh teacher of my friend Hywel from Welshpool (he's basically the most Welsh creature alive...). 'And there's a fair bit of fire and brimstone in the Welsh character,' she warns. Wales's most famous poet Dylan Thomas developed his own declamatory style after being inspired by his aunt Dosie's minister husband, the Reverend David Rees. His sermons were so packed with passion that Dylan began to ruminate on the power of preaching and the uniquely Welsh quality of *hwyl*, which he embraced and utilised, notably in 'The Peaches'. Today, *hwyl* is entirely secular and free from moral undertones, but traces of Welsh ministers' bombasticism and a tendency towards the theatrical remain. 'A Welsh person of a certain age will turn straight to the deaths column in the paper and say, "Who's died?"' Diane tells me. 'It's just part of the Welsh psyche – that melancholic strain that we quite enjoy,' she explains. 'We like drama.'

The Welsh prioritise the arts with nationwide festivals of poetry, literature and performance called *eisteddfodau* dating back to the 12th century. Every child will experience *eisteddfodau* in school, then there are youth *eisteddfodau*, village *eisteddfodau*, regional *eisteddfodau*, national *eisteddfodau* – even international *eisteddfodau* with outposts of the Welsh institution set up in Argentina and Patagonia in the 19th century. 'You can see the *hwyl* in full force at *eisteddfodau*,' Diane tells me, explaining that on a national level these are very prestigious and people compete to win 'a carved chair and crown'. I'm just about to say that this sounds very *Game of Thrones* when Diane tells me that 'the Welsh really celebrate intellectualism' and I think better of it. The Welsh are so damn cerebral that until recently, a page of one of the country's weekly newspapers was dedicated to poetry technique and construction. You wouldn't get that in the rest of the UK.

Learning has always been prioritised in Wales as having inherent value, but education was also seen as a way to spare your children the hardships of having to work down the mine. In the Industrial Revolution, coal replaced wood as the staple resource, and mining became the biggest single employer in Wales. A hazardous profession thanks to collapses and accidents, miners were also at risk from respiratory conditions and muscular problems from working in cramped seams. Then the rise of oil sparked the beginning of the end for mining in Wales and pit closures followed – despite the famous 1984 miners' strike, which was unceremoniously crushed by Margaret Thatcher.

'There's a huge amount of respect for the work the miners did and for their traditions,' says Diane, '– and when the mines closed, a lot of the close-knit communities and whole social structures went, too, which was a tragedy. But the work itself was hard and dangerous, so miners always wanted to educate their kids so they could have a better life.' Thanks to these adversities and Wales's sense of being a little nation next to a much bigger, more powerful ex-imperial neighbour, there has always been a strong community spirit and sense of solidarity amongst the Welsh. There's a tradition of trade unions, life-long Labour voters, and progressive schemes such as universal healthcare that eventually morphed into the creation of the NHS under Welshman Aneurin Bevan. 'We're also strongly non-conformist and bloody minded,' Hywel adds. I flipping love the Welsh.

On top of an eternity of sharp-elbowed resilience, the Welsh have made a concerted effort to preserve their traditions in recent years. Since 1992, it's been compulsory to learn Welsh in schools and you will never meet anyone from Wales who isn't insanely proud of their dragon-crested heritage. 'There's something about our home – our country – that means a hell of a lot to people in Wales,' says Diane. She furnishes me with further linguistic gems from the Welsh language to prove her patriotic point. There's *cynefin*, a noun meaning the relationship one has to the place where one was born, the place one is most at home, or the place

where one feels one ought to live. Then there's the wonderfully named *milltir sgwâr* or 'square mile' – a phrase used to define your patch of land or the location that tugs on your heartstrings. 'Where you're from is very important in Wales,' says Ben, who tells me that his family can trace its roots back to the same 10-square kilometre patch of South Wales since the 1700s ('we didn't like to travel far').

Ben's family may have been more rooted than most, but the impulse to stay in the motherland is one that all Welsh people experience to a degree. 'We have something called *hiraeth*,' Diane tells me, ' – a homesickness-type feeling of deep love and nostalgia for our country – or even a mythical idea of our country'. I'm envisaging dragons (because: 'Wales') but Diane goes on to describe a chest-expanding passion for one's country that I can't quite relate to as a mere jolly Englishwoman. 'It's *hwyl*,' she tells me, pinpointing the heart swell of *hiraeth* and reiterating: 'It isn't a soft, easy sort of pleasurable feeling: it's a walloping big fervour or zest for life that's just very...Welsh!' Or, as my friend Ben puts it, 'we do everything with welly.' Amen to that.

HOW TO EXPERIENCE *HWYL*

1

Fill your sails; operate at full pelt; and embrace life's
highs and lows (valley-style).

2

Sing whenever possible, hankies at the ready.

3

Celebrate education and intellectualism – because it's for all of us,
no matter what age we are or what our social background.
And if *hwyl* is about living life with welly, we should always want to
know more about the world.

4

Cherish your home and the people in it. And know that it's OK to really,
really miss it when you're away from it. The *hiraeth* is all part of the ride.

ACKNOWLEDGEMENTS

I would like to thank Anna Power, Kate Hewson and Lisa Highton for making this book happen and to Naomi Wilkinson for making it a thing of beauty. Thanks to everyone who has contributed their stories and experiences as well as the wonderfully well connected and insightful Ali Budjanovcanin, Ian Busch, James Mendes, Kath Poulsen, Tony Haile, Tara Wike, Chris Chinaloy, Rachel Taylor, Frank Skilbeck, Jack Burnford, Nic Ross, Rita Ward, Fenella Charity and Katie Freeman.

ABOUT THE AUTHOR

Helen Russell is a journalist and the bestselling author of *The Year of Living Danishly*, *Leap Year* and *Gone Viking*.

Formerly editor of MarieClaire.co.uk, she now lives in Denmark and works as a Scandinavia correspondent for the *Guardian*, as well as writing features for *The Times*, The *Observer*, *Grazia*, *Stylist* and the *Independent*. She has also written for *The Wall Street Journal* and wrote a long-standing column on Denmark for the *Telegraph*.

Also by Helen Russell
The Year of Living Danishly
Leap Year
Gone Viking